CRIME, COMMUNITY AND POLICE

CRIME COMMUNITY AND POLICE

V. K. MOHANAN

Gian Publishing House

DELHI-110007

GIAN PUBLISHING HOUSE
29/6 SHAKTI NAGAR, DELHI-110007

ISBN 81-212-0107-1

PRINTED IN INDIA

*Published by Gian Publishing House, Delhi-110007
and Printed at Suman Printers, 9 Puri Street,
Maujpur, Delhi-110053*

PREFACE

This work is the result of an extensive study conducted in the State of Kerala relating the role of police in their interaction with criminals and community members. Studies on police-community relations are assuming greater importance these days especially from the point of view of the rehabilitation of the criminal in society and police reform.

I express my sincere gratitude and indebtedness to my supervisor Dr G. Narayana Pillay, Reader in Sociology, University of Kerala, for his valuable guidance and advice at each stage of the study without which this study would not have been completed. Dr Pillay's instructive criticisms and penetrating suggestions were the major guidelines in carrying out this study.

I wish to express my sincere thanks to the Inspector General of Police, Inspector General of Prisons, Superintendents of Central and Subjails in my study. Superintendents of Police in the respective areas and Sub-Inspectors of Police who had been highly helpful to me during my fieldwork for this study.

I would like to thank greatly my respondents for having co-operated in giving their valuable ideas and opinions to my enquiries.

My sincere thanks to Dr. P.K.B. Nayar, Professor and Head, Department of Sociology for providing all facilities for conducting the work.

Lastly I wish to add that I am greatly thankful to my friends who had been sincerely helping me at different stages of my research on this problem.

V.K. MOHANAN

CONTENTS

1

INTRODUCTION

The Problem of Criminal Behaviour

Social norms are always two-sided. A prescription may point out the prevalence of a prohibition and vice versa. Important norms generally relate to crucial social values and therefore the highest degree of consensus depends on them. The isolation of these we generally call deviant behaviour, and crime is an example of this. A crime then is an offence against the entire community rather than against any individual within the community. There are three main conceptions of crime—the legal, the behavioural and the conduct norm definition. Under these factors the emergent role of the police in relaton to crime as a law enforcing agency is highly important. Equally significant is the part played by the community in the crime process. In society these factors function differently in different conditions. Emergence of new and varied policies on police administration, implementation of programmes on crime investigation, judicial procedures, correctional services, and rehabilitative programmes are recent developments in the area of crime treatment. Added to this the emerging role of the community and its preparedness for the new venture towards the issue have initiated new and varied developments and observations in modern society. In the context of increasing complexity in the structure, growing crime rate and population growth in the society, concern about the problem of the exact relationship between crime, community and the police has grown all the more in our society.

Under these circumstances, it is pertinent to ask the question : How do the police behave towards criminals ? What is the attitude of different official groups of police towards criminals ? To what extent do the police in Kerala have professional enthusiasm in the context of police-criminal interactions ? How does the police in Kerala react to the conditions of internal corruption ? How does the community around respond or react to the police-criminal interaction ? How does the police respond to the community ? These issues are highly relevant in a democratic society where the discipline, the law enforcement and the social order attempt to conform to the needs of the society in a more ideal manner. A thorough understanding of the mechanism of relationship between criminal behaviour, the police and the community will be able to provide answers to the above questions.

This is precisely the subject matter of the present study. It attempts to explain the different processes of interaction and influences between the criminals, the police and community members within which the triad functions in society.

Crime, Police and Community

Studies on crime behaviour have developed in two main channels. Firstly, the mechanistic, situational or dynamic and secondly, the historical or genetic approaches devised by Sutherlend. This covered more about the individual actor himself or herself in the situation. Sutherlend's theory of 'differential association' emphasizes that criminal behaviour is learned in a process of social interaction. R.K. Merton and Cohen emphasized the approach of a systematic classification of the responses of the members of a group to deviance. Since the change over from the classical school associated with Cesare Bonesana and Marchese de Beccaria, the Italian noblemen, through the neo-classical school and subsequently the positive school associated with the Italian professor, Cesare Lombroso, we notice a remarkable transition from the individual centred approach to a viewpoint where environmental influences were given more emphasis.

Subsequent developments in the methodology of criminological studies centred on the concern for the offender as an individual and the influences of the environment on his behaviour. Within the programme of environmental approach which emphasizes the influences external to the individual on crime, Taft refers to objective approaches as the effective method. He uses the term in the sense of 'derived from without'. George B. Vold has referred to 'group behaviour theories' which centre on crime as an aspect of group phenomena in which the particular characteristics of specific individuals may be quite incidental (Vold, 1958 : 308).

However, the influence of further developments, more especially by the emergence of the ecological approach propounded by the scientific school of sociology headed by Park and Burgess, a new focus on the community and its impact on the individual in the context of criminal characteristics is highly significant. Though all these approaches deal with the situations of crime and criminality in an exhaustive manner, our study is more closely related to the latter model, as the ecological or environmental factors and influences are given more weight in the study through its emphasis on the police-criminal relationships in the context of community interaction. Hence, in the following sections we give a short account of the approaches to the study of criminal behaviour and the police in the community set-up.

Every crime involves a situation and a social definition of that situation. A crime *ipso facto* implies a disturbance in a social relationship and a social definition as to what such a disturbance is (Elliot and Merrill, 1961 : 106). From the point of view of its causation, scholars have attempted to explain this kind of anti-social behaviour in different ways. Robert Merton, Richard Cloward, Ohlin and Taft explained that criminal behaviour arises due to socially induced stresses. Merton indicated in his theory on the basis of disjunction between cultural and social systems of society that deviancy is the result of reaction towards activity or change generated in the actor. Merton thinks that an anomic situation arises when disjunction between goals and means causes strain which, in turn, leads to the weakening of man's commitment to the culturally prescribed goals or institutionalized means, that is to a state of anomie and it is this state which leads to anti-social behaviour. Strain, frustration, depression, etc. are not the result of any one of those, but are the result of the relationship among all these factors. Thus a disjunction between goals and institutionalized means can arise either because of escalation of the goals or because of the contraction of the definition of legitimate ways of achieving them. Though Merton has attempted to explain deviant behaviour and its manifestation through crime etc., his theory is incomplete in the sense that it explains only the role of the situation and not of the personality factors involved in the affair.

Criminologists like Sutherlend, Clifford Shaw, Cyril Burt, Frederic Thrasher and Charles Booth have emphasized the role of various social deprivations as the cause of crime in society. But Lombrose explained criminal behaviour in terms of physical characteristics of offenders and concluded that criminals were born (Lombroso, 1911 : 17). Ferri supported the above view that individuals committed crimes due to inherited atavistic or physical anomalies (Enrico 1917 : 12). Goring refuted this view, and felt that inferior physique and mental retardation were responsible for an individual's criminal behaviour. Hooton and Sheldon Gluek too held the same opinion in this regard. Sutherlend maintained that from a personal point of view, criminals are criminals because of their differential association with others which initiate them into criminal activities. From the point of view of society, he felt that it is social disorganization which explains crime. He also concluded that personality traits do not explain crime satisfactorily. There are nevertheless certain factors which seem to characterize persons convicted of crime (Edwin, 1949 : 21). Very often crime is a product of a large number and a great variety of factors and these factors cannot now and perhaps ever be organized into general propositions which have no exception (Venugopal, 1962 : 10). Mabel Elliot was of the opinion that crime is a legal problem and defines it as any act or failure to act, which is forbidden or prescribed by law, the failure to abide by such law being punishable by fine, imprisonment, banishment, death or other punitive treatment as the particular state may prescribe (Elliot, 1952 : 13-14).

To Walter Reckless, crime is not a genetic behavioural phenomenon but can be explained only as a different order of behaviour. He emphasized what he called social vulnerabilities of the individual and categoric risks for official action. The former are the weaknesses of the individual when confronted with a situation which may precipitate criminal behaviour (Reckless, 1943 : 137). In this context it may be pointed out that crime must be recognized clearly as not being a unitary phenomenon but as consisting of many kinds of behaviour occurring under many different situations also. No single theory, therefore, should be expected to provide the explanations for the many varieties of behaviour involved.

Any condition that leads to the weakening of social bonds or to the development of conflict and dissension in place of cultural uniformity and homogeneity, may so weaken motives for conformity that individuals are willing to commit criminal acts. Such conditions are found in modern society. Increasing social differentiation and heterogeneity may lead to the disruption of social relationships among groups occupying statuses and engaged in different functions, even though there may be stable bonds within such groups (Wheeler, 1967 : 214). The predisposing factors on criminal behaviour include some anomalies in the structure of the family unit, ecological and economic factors, social change by industrialization, urbanization, migration, social disorganization and anomic. Culture conflict may apply to all or to some of those predisposing factors and at various stages of their genesis (Marvin, 1968 : 59). In this connection, William and John McCard believe that there is a strong emotional factor in criminality. They also found that absence of parental love led to adult criminality even when these grown-ups had no juvenile record (William and McCard, 1959 :164-5).

Earlier studies showed a high crime rate among young men who were foreign born. Most criminals today are native born. Race, however, is significantly related to crime. (Elliot and Merrill, 1961 : 132). The discrepancy between culturally prescribed aspirations and social opportunities, in other words the 'anomie' situation, is most frequently shown as the fundamental cause of high probabilities of crime in society (Scheffer, 1968 : 83). The role of women in modern society probably has something to do with low crime rate among women. The average woman is a success if she is a successful wife and mother. She usually does not strive for economic success. Her goals are more often emotional than economic. In fact it is when her emotional life is upset that she is most likely to become a criminal as the analysis of marital status and crime rate indicates. In any event women do not commit as many crimes as men, apparently because they have less motivation to commit crimes (Elliot, 1952 : viii).

Deviant behaviour is common and no society is an exception to this. However, cultural, social and structural variations may vary with respect to the nature of the problem. Hence, it is the *prima facie* duty of the society to control this type of behaviour in order to enable its members to lead a stable and normal life. Society has its own machinery for the above purpose. Criminal justice system bears the explicit responsibility for preventing and controlling crime in society. Thus, as Kerper states, the criminal justice system is the institution charged with direct responsibility for the prevention and control of crime (Kerper, 1972 : 1).

The criminal justice system recognizes that the efficiency of the legal machinery depends basically on the quality of the initial work done by the police (Barnes and Teeters, 1966 : 211). Prevention and control of crime is the basic duty of the police. They are designed and established for this purpose. Hence police, in the most common meaning of the term, is a body of trained men who are organized to maintain public order, preserve liberty and make life and property of the citizen secure against assault, burglary, theft and the depredations (Ahmad, 1957 : 76).

The role of the police in modern society in preserving law and order in the community around which it functions is extremely important. Their efficiency, behaviour, discipline, etc. affect a lot in the fulfiling of their duties which are assigned to them by society. The term 'police' thus refers primarily to agents of the state whose function is the maintenance of law and order and especially the enforcement of the regular criminal code (Sutherlend and Cressey, 1965 : 330).

As Johnson states, the police represent the legal system because they apply the coercive power of the state and administer the intake of persons processed by the system of criminal justice (Elmer, 1968 : 361). In a welfare state, the police assumes various roles. They are : (1) to prevent crime and disorder, (2) to recognize always that the power of the police to fulfil their functions and duties is dependent on public approval of their existence, actions, and behaviour and on their ability to maintain public respect, (3) to effect willing co-operation of the public in the task of securing observance of law, (4) to recognize always the extent to which the co-operation of the public can be secured. The extent to which these roles can be fulfilled diminishes proportionately the necessity of the use of physical force and compulsion for achieving police objectives (Gupta, 1957 : 97).

While discussing the role of the police in society, Alan R. Coffey defined the basic functions of the police as prevention of crime, detection of crimes that have been committed, identification of the person or persons responsible for crimes, apprehension of the person or persons responsible for crimes, detection of the suspected offender or offenders for processing by the judiciary, and presentation of evidence to the prosecutor (Coffer, 1975 : 95). As the police has a definite role in the maintenance of public order in the society their behaviour influences greatly the performance of their duties. Reactions of the police towards criminals, suspectors, witnesses, and to the general public play a significant role in the maintenance of law and order in society. It has been quite often felt that police as a law enforcing machinery of the government, vested with numerous powers, often act lawlessly towards the criminals and to the general public with whom they come into contact.

From another point of view, it may be pointed out that the ability of the police to perform their duties is dependent upon public approval of police existence, actions, behaviour and the ability of the police to secure and maintain public respect (Louis, 1977 : 4). However, the general complaint against the police force is the excessive use of force on suspects and others. Policemen also often confess to the use of third-degree methods against suspects in police custody but their argument is that any method that deals with hard criminals cannot be first degree. This image and reality of police behaviour makes the common man shudder when one talks of the use of third-degree methods in police work (Sharma, 1981 : 70). Thus, the proper behaviour of the policeman many a time depends upon the circumstances in which he is exposed to do his duty.

On issues relating to police behaviour, an important aspect which very often comes to mind is the one relating to police brutality. What actually a citizen regards as police brutality, many policemen consider necessary for law enforcement. Hence, what is proper and what is brutal, it need hardly be pointed out, is more a matter of judgement about what someone did than a description of what police do. Any practice that degrades their status, that restricts their freedom, that annoys or harasses them, or that uses physical force is frequently seen as unnecessary and unwarranted (Radzinowicz and Wolfgang, 1971 : 148). According to the police, there is no first-degree method of dealing with hardened criminals. Conversely it is more than true that no civilized society, and still less a democratic society, can tolerate the use of third-degree methods of torture, abuse and violence on suspects in the process of sorting out real criminals. It violates the dignity of the individual (Sharma, 1981 : 282).

Hence it is an art and a fine art to handle a criminal sympathetically and properly. Here the behavioural patterns of the police become very significant and it may also be noted that they may vary widely on the basis of the nature of situations. A section of the people who are disciplined and overwhelmed with power and authority are quite likely to have a prejudiced attitude towards others. Though they are the people who are trained in a systematic manner intended for the welfare of the general public, their sub-cultural nature tempts them to act and react to the society in a quite different fashion. Here the individualistic and the official fallacies come into operation. It will be very interesting to examine the wide varieties of this kind of behaviour to the members of the society with whom the police come into contact, i.e. the suspects, offenders and the general public. Under these circumstances in this study we have made an attempt to examine the nature of police behaviour towards the offenders and the public in the hope of getting more details on their efficieny and their profession as they are the persons whose primary duty is to control and prevent crime and to maintain law and order in the society. Police behaviour during the span of their official career may be different to different community members varying with the individual qualities and capacities of the policeman ; the last also have a definite role in the controlling of crime.

Theoretically a policeman is a servant of the law, practically he is a servant of the police minister in the state. He will be called upon to control crime by hock or crook, waive cases, withdraw cases, prosecute cases, make out cases, maintain dossiers on rivals and report on them and face agitations for doing all this (Ghosh, 1981 : 82). These situations are very common everywhere in modern society. Under these circumstances it is true that police investigations on crime, by and large, trace the conventional paths. There has been very little training input for the investigating officers to diagnose the sociology of crime and pathologies of violence in the changing psychology of the weaker sections in the midst of criminal situations and provocative surroundings (Sharma, 1981 : 215). These factors may well influence the police behaviour towards offenders at times. As stated by Whyte, "The primary function of the police and the police department is not the enforcement of law but the regulation of illegal activities" (Elliot and Merrill, 1961 : 533).

The behaviour of the police is sometimes criticized by the public in many ways regarding the way they deal with the criminals or with the suspects and the general public. The tone of their language and the use of excessive force, etc. are faced with severe criticism. They are frequently blamed for outmoded methods of investigation and lack of knowledge of law, both of which lead to failures in courts. The force thus if used by the police may be explained in various terms. It may be explained by police culture than by the policeman's race, and also the victim of excessive force is usually a lower-class man of either race ; whether or not a policeman uses force unnecessarily depends upon the social setting in which the encounter takes place (Radzinoviez and Wolfgeng, 1971 : 157). Likewise age, educational and economic background and other external factors of the police officer also influence his behaviour towards those with whom he comes into contact during official work. As Sharma says, the younger generation of police officers at all levels is relatively more enlightened and is imbued with democratic values of self respect, individual freedom and professional commitment. To him the political atmosphere surfeit with corruption and nihilism gets reflected in the day-to-day behaviour of demoralized constabulary (Sharma, 1981 : 135-7).

As stated above, it is very difficult for the police officer to be natural in his behaviour towards criminals or suspects or even to the public. Many factors outside his profession influence him in his actions than his own individual differences. The political set-up of the state, influences from higher sources of bureaucracy, etc. have a definite role in this scene. In a period of rapid social change, it is important to ask how an officer can steer a course of neutrality if he cannot rely upon the principles of full enforcement of the law against all citizens regardless of social status or racial status (Radelet, 1977: 225). The influence on the police by the politicians has been discussed by several officials and criminologists in the police profession. In the case of police organization even, they cannot be left on their own because the job of policing requires policy direction and discretionary interpretation subject to the overall control of the judiciary of the country. Consequently, in modern situations, the working conditions of the police personnel may also influence a great deal in their behaviour towards others. The circumstances, environment and service conditions, etc. have a definite role in moulding the behaviour of the policeman inside and outside his sphere of work. In the words of M.M. Singh : "The state police constantly needs a lot to be desired in terms of its professional behaviour and still more in the field of amelioration of working conditions of policemen, which alone can ensure recruitment of the light kind" (Singh, 1962 : 12).

It may be added here that the growth of politician-policemen in recent years has affected the discipline and loyalty in the police force (Ghosh, 1981 : 102). It has been aptly indicated by Sharma that the political upheavals and social disorganization accentuated by development and modernization, have strengthened the Indian police in its negative role with very little time, skill and vision of a positive police, sharing the excitement of change plus growth called development (Sharma, 1981 : 13). Dissatisfaction in the profession is very much related to one's further performance in the profession.

Improper conduct and rude behaviour of the police are often the result of unsatisfactory working conditions. The merit of officers or subordinate officials for promotion on the basis of convictions secured is also to a great extent responsible for the use of third-degree methods and padding by the police. It is also to be noted that when police operate under corrupt conditions, law enforcement suffers and the police service becomes a defensive manoeuvre rather than an effective law enforcement machinery (Ghosh, 1981 : 90-1). Often the police employ lawless methods (including third-degree) or prolonged and brutal interviews, make false arrests, including arrests on suspicion and tap wires to secure evidence. Many police sectors believe that they "have to break the law to secure justice". Where police are corrupt, the situation is much worse since justice becomes a mockery and the police are literally 'aiders and abettors' of crime (Elliot and Merrill, 1961 : 555).

Police are considered as the visual representatives of the government. They represent a pre-condition for the establishment and maintenance of law and order. The political set-up in any country and the establishment of government also depend upon the police and their behaviour to the general public under the rule. The role of the police in a democratic set-up is too strategic and extremes of police behaviour may sometimes lead even to the collapse of governments or at least severe criticism from the opposition.

In order to execute the duties and responsibilities that are assigned to the police force, their professional equipment must be modified in such a way as to meet any situation of emergency. Justice Krishna Iyer observed that when everything else seems changing police and judiciary in India have been least susceptible to social and political change (Krishna Iyer, 1981 : 129-36). This statement points to the need for a rapid change in the police policy and profession. The efficiency of the police in any society will be according to the law and order situation and the rate of crime in the community around them. The test of police efficiency is the absence of crime and disorder, not the visible evidence of police action in dealing with them (Louis, 1977 : 4).

In the real assessment of the professional orientation of the police, the characteristics of individual policemen, selection, education, training, service conditions like scope of promotion, job satisfaction, modern equipments in police stations, better facilities of service, etc. have a definite function in their role performance. The policeman really has two role models from which to choose, he can conceive of himself as a rule enforcer or as a guardian of peace (Gorden, 1975 : 488).

By police professionalism Wilson means an institutionalization of rules and norms expressing, not feelings of group separateness, but an external body of 'expert' knowledge about 'correct' police work (James, 1963: 189-216). Hence, for a good police department good personnel, careful selection, adequate training and appropriate remuneration of police officers are essential (Sutherlend and Cressey, 1978 : 411).

Studies have shown that the prevailing training methods and the actual content of training do not contribute much towards inculcating qualities of good judgement, prudence and common sense among police recruits. The peculiar kind of responsibilities and duties the police officials are entrusted with and the nature of their work which isolates them from other spheres of life tend to form a group alien from others.

Yet another drawback of the police in their routine work is preferential treatment, favouritism, nepotism and even corruption in matters relating to distribution of duties, grant of leave, allotment of family quarters, examination tests, grant of rewards and punishments, transfers and postings, etc. at lower levels (Ghosh, 1981 : 104).

Senior police officials complain, and perhaps very righly so, about the inadequacy of members commensurate to the prescribed strengths of their outposts, police stations and special agencies in the department. The work entrusted to them and the manpower provided for the same are not commensurate with each other. Among other factors significant here, the nature of the government and its policies to a great extent influence the performance of the police and their duties. The way in which they handle the situation also affects the general police of the government. Hence the police system under a paternalistic government where the later alone should initiate and regulate basic change assumes a significant role (Chinnappa, 1972 : 1-12).

Edward George writing about Indian police, in his work on *The Police on the Urban Frontier*, says that there is no other country in the world claiming to be civilized in which more is expected of the police and less is given to them in the way of encouragement and material advantages (George, 1968 : 29). But the functional image of the police in India is quite bad and people of all strata hold it in low esteem also. As regards the role performance of police, only a very small section of the community accepts that the police are helpful. A large section of the Indian society feels that the police functions with partiality, favouritism and injustice. In their judgement the police are professionally incompetent, cruel and corrupt (Srivastava, 1972 : 243-63). If this is so, a neglected police force can never be a good law enforcement machinery which the citizens want. A demoralized and diffident police administration cannot act as the bulwark of law and order and social stability (Ghosh, 1981 : 98-126).

In spite of all these defects it is to be admitted that the police service the community around with utmost care. As revealed by the Royal Commission in Britain in paying for our policeman we are paying for our own security. We are, in effect, insuring ourselves against disorder and crime. In return we are entitled to demand the maintenance of those high standards of efficiency and courtesy which have made the police admired and respected around the world (Ghosh, 1981 : 109). In a general sense two types of police forces are found in the world today, i.e. people's police and ruler-appointed police. The best example of people's police is to be seen in Britain and Japan where police forces are the agents of the law of the land. The ruler-appointed police is found in totalitarian countries like Russia where they are the attitude sanctions of the State and are regularly used as such. In all countries with democratic governments, a large part of the work of the "people's police is carried on with the assistance of the public and of an independent press, both of which are free to comment and criticise as they feel inclined" (Ibid., 1981 : 94).

Bayley in his book *The Police and Political Development in India* has brought out the 'police' as the employees of the community. To him the special purpose of it is to ensure that the community's laws are observed. The police may be distinguished from other agents of the community who enforce law, employ force or wear uniforms by (a) having an exclusively domestic mandate and (b) being the initial point of contact between citizen and enforcement machinery (Bayley, 1969 : 4). It may be understood here that the police in order to fulfil their duties and responsibilities need the help and co-operation of the community in which they work. The degree of co-operation extended by the public to the police in their work depends more on the mutual interaction between them in the society. Hence the role of police in preventing lawlessness would have mainly two aspects : (a) negative, consisting of curbing socially destructive tendencies directly (b) positive, consisting of arousing constructive tendencies and thus checking destructive tendencies indirectly (Saran, 1957 : 85).

Public co-operation is always necessary in the enforcement of major laws and minor regulations which help in the successful administration of the police department (Bhardwaj, 1978 : 34). Hence, the degree of co-operation of the public that can be secured diminishes proportionately with the necessity for using physical force and compulsion in achieving police objectives. They should maintain a relationship with the public that gives reality to the historic tradition that the police are the public and the public are the police. The police are the only members of the public who are paid to give full-time attention to duties which are incumbent on every citizen in the interest of the community welfare (Redelet, 1977 : 4).

If a police officer is to be effective in every neighbourhood, he must understand the habits and the culture of the people in the area he patrols (Bent and Rossum, 1976 : 27). With an understanding of the culture and behavioural patterns of the people around, the police will enable them to maintain law and order situation more efficiently. This is according to the sociological theory which maintains that crime is the result of various social elements operating in the social environment. These elements are culture, social control, primary and secondary groups, social process, socialization, social change, social disorganization, status, role and personality of the individual (Adwani, 1978 : 26). Hence, crime rates will differ according to the extent of disjuncture between the goals persons internalize and their socially structured opportunities for achieving them (Becker, 1967 : 221).

Increasing trend of urbanization, a characteristic of every modern society, has great influence on the conditions and on police-community relations. Not only do the congestion and poor living conditions found in some urban areas tend to breed crime, but the anonymity fostered by large cities often leads to citizen apathy. An indifferent public that fails to support law enforcement dooms the efforts of the police successfully to prevent and control crime (Coffey, 1975 : 122).

Thus police-community relations have to be maintained with the attitude of the police towards themselves and segments of the community, and the attitude of segments of the community towards themselves and the police. Generally, police-community relations in the present context include dealings with problems created by the changing relations between social change and social control. It also depends on what the police expect from the community and what the community expects from the police. What the police do, then, and how they do it are vitally important considerations in the status of the relationship (Redelet, 1977 : 23-32). Police-citizen relationship in all societies is essentially a situation dependent upon two major variables obtaining at a given period of history in a particular society. These are : (1) the ideological values of the political system which the rulers of the country profess or prefer to practise in relation to the bulk of the citizenry ; and (2) the operating socio-cultural norms, which tend to condition the bureaucratic ethos of the administrative structures, more so in a developing society (Sharma, 1981 : 168). Police are considered as the leading edge of government regulation. What they do is part and parcel of government's activity. Police and government could no more be separated than knife and knife-edge (Bayley, 1969 : 11). They are society's regulators imbued with power denied to every one else. This creates around them an aura of apprehension, of anxiety and fear.

Hence, police roles are primarily determined by three factors : societal norms; mores and influences ; the individual policeman's discretion ; and the level of urbanization of society. Society's norms and mores are consequential for police roles because a particular society or culture will incorporate into its legal structure what it views as proper police jurisdiction (Bent and Rossum, 1976 : 15).

The public attitude towards the police is heavily influenced by actual contacts with the police and is stressed in the observations of a number of theories. Wirths stresses that specific attitude towards the police reflects an interplay of society, family, culture and personality ; therefore these attitudes are complex (Wirths, 1958 : 52).

Police-community relations have a direct bearing on the character of life in the cities and on the ability of the community to maintain stability and solve its problems. At the same time the ability of the police department to deal with crime depends in large part on its relation with the citizenry (Coffey, 1975 : 128).

With regard to the extent of commitment of the police to the community, the breadth of police roles includes among police responsibilities such things as the creation and maintenance of a feeling of security in the community, the resolution of conflict, the protection of constitutional guarantees and the helping of those who cannot care for themselves (Bent and Rossum, 1976 : 4). Police work and police-community relations are of extraordinary importance in our society because police officers are authorized by the community they serve to exercise extraordinary power under certain circumstances (Radelet, 1977: 76). Banton finds that the policeman obtains public co-operation and enjoys public esteem because he enforces standards accepted by the community. This gives him a special role of considerable moral authority.

Many a time the police officer is the product of a particular background or social environment. This includes certain experiences and certain social institutional influences, namely family, social class, nationality, ethnic and cultural factors, race, religion, education, parental occupations, political views and the like. The combination of these influences produces certain attitudes, beliefs, and values in the individual police officer as it does with any other person (Ibid., p. 72). Goalhart has supported this view, and has stated that the surest way of obtaining public co-operation is to demonstrate efficiency in criminal investigation and crime prevention. If the people have faith that the police will be able to accomplish these essential tasks, they will be more willing to offer assistance even to the point of enduring infringements of their liberty (Royal Commission on the Police, 1962: 157-81).

It is essential that the police executive must be skilful in maintaining relationship within the community power structure whereby the resource needs of his agency are made known to decision-makers, resource allocations are obtained and police problems can be communicated in a style conducive to obtaining community support (Radelet, 1977 : 430). Lack of competency on the part of the police may be as great a hazard to the community as corrupt police. It is also true that police protection cannot be assured without police who have adequate intelligence and education. A policeman also needs to be physically strong. He should be acquainted with the places where crimes tend to be committed. He should be trained in police techniques and criminology. Relatively few police forces pass such qualifications (Elliot and Merrill, 1961:556).

From the viewpoint of the community, it has been noted that nowadays the police have found the public to be indifferent to police problems. One of the reactions which the criticism and indifference have produced is organized effort to develop friendly understanding with the public. In this effort the police department has established a public relation division and has attempted to develop methods which will reduce the amount of irritation provoked by existing procedures (Sutherlend and Cressey, 1965: 352). Very often a given social system is more or less functional depending upon the quality of these relationships in exactly the same way as a community or a large police department (both complicated and multiple social systems in themselves) are more or less functional as measured against their purposes. Hence the relationship within the criminal justice system between police and other functionaries is to be viewed from their structural limitations.

The widespread general complaint against the police is the prevalence of corruption. The complainant comes more into contact with the police than any person in the other department. To Lawrence Sherman, "The problem of police corruption is merely a slice of a larger problem of official corruption in American Society" (Sherman, 1974:1).

Herman Goldstein says that corruption is endemic to policing. Difficult as it is to stamp out all corruption, it is clear that it can be reduced and in some specific situations, eliminated (Goldstein, 1975:52).

Bracey assigns eight explicit functions to the phenomenon of police corruption. Three of these are intimately connected with the preservation of a police sub-culture that is quite distinct from others in a society. The existence of a police sub-culture is well documented. Its principal characteristics are usually described as intense peer-group feelings of solidarity, a cynical attitude towards many of the laws which members of the sub-culture are required to uphold and towards many of the people they are obliged to protect, and a feeling of alienation from the rest of the community. The sub-culture and the values and behaviour of its members are usually described in terms of the nature of the police role in society and the defensive attitude of the police towards the outside world. Bracey again analyses the functionality of corruption in order to explain how it helps to maintain those features of the sub-culture (Bracey, 1976:12).

Misner defines police corruption as the abuse or illegal use of office for the direct and indirect pecuniary gain of the individual policemen (Misner, 1975 : 46). Judging from the various preconditions of the phenomenon. It may also mean the misuse of authority by a police officer in a manner designed to produce personal gain for himself or for others (Goldstein, 1975:3).

To Barker and Roebuck, "Corruption can assume the dimensions of any type of prescribed behaviour engaged in by a law enforcement officer who receives or expects to receive by virtue of his official position, any unauthorized material reward or gain" (Barker and Roebuck, 1974:8-9). According to

McMullen, "A public official is corrupt if he accepts money or money's worth for doing something that he is under a duty not to do or to exercise a legitimate description for improper reasons" (McMullen, 1961:183-4).

Research Findings

Several studies have pointed out the salient features of police-criminal relationships. A large part of them deal with the findings in relation to the role of community also. Reckless C. Walter examined the behaviour of the police towards the community in his work on crime problem and found out that the members of the lower class in any society are more defenseless and have fewer resources and less influence than members of the middle and upper classes. Other things being equal, the police are more likely to suspect a lower-class person rather than an upper-class person. They would arrest a lower-class person on suspicion more readily than a middle or upper-class person. They are more active in areas where lower-class persons reside (Walter, 1971:110).

Singh yound in his study on criminal justice and the police that indifferent treatment and way of behaviour affect the real duties and ends desired from the police officials. The absence of trained police staff and popular co-operation in criminal investigation make the prosecution stories weak in cases involving the weaker sections of society. Whether it is weak vs. weak or weak vs. weaker, corrupt practices and political pressures in investigations can easily cause interference in the administration of criminal justice (Singh, 1967:153-75).

A Rajasthan police study team in their study came across the finding that the police harassment is enormous on the criminals. According to their finding, corruption is rampant at the lower levels and nobody listens at higher levels. During the course of investigation, police behaviour is generally crude and use of third-degree methods against suspects is the common experience. Investigating officers throw feelers for graft and those who cannot afford it are physically harassed and their womenfolk insulted. The police rarely cares to put its best into solving a criminal case where the poor are involved (National Police Commission, 1979).

With regard to the Indian police, Bayley found from his work on police and political developments in India that the work of the police is arduous, often directly and unpleasant and sometimes dangerous. "Indian police are always subject to call ... Nightwork is a standard feature of their life... They are not paid for overtime work. They often work on holidays and during festivals... They are expected to risk their lives... And finally the responsibility thrust upon them is enormous" (Bayley, 1969:305).

Radelet observed from an IACP survey that the motivation of the police officer to join the department also plays a significant part in his effective discharge of duties. In one survey it was seen that 54 per cent of the policewomen came into this profession almost by accident. They had tried several jobs and finally settled for the police force (Radelet, 1977: 104).

Skolnick (1968) observed in his work on the relationship between police and urban Ghetto that the problem of police in a democratic society is not merely a matter of obtaining new police cars or more sophisticated equipment or communication systems or of recruiting men who have to their credit more years of education.

Reddy and Sheshadri (1972) in their study on training police officers in developing society observed that the outdoor training of the junior functionaries certainly prepares them for arduous jobs of a hazardous manner. But it runs the risk of brutalizing their instincts for finer things in life and society (Reddy and Sheshadri, 1972:141-51).

While discussing the importance and the need for improving professional standards of the police, Sharma derived from his study on police polity and people in India that sophisticated qualified incumbents in the civil police, especially in the lower ranks, are lacking. This indirectly indicated the qualitative deficiency of police equipment (Sharma, 1981 : 273). On similar lines, Subramanian also found out from his study on police organizations that a lack of positive vista and obsession with negative policing have deepened dilemmas of policing as a profession (Subramanian, 1964: 134-6).

S.C. Misra observed in his work on police administration that the average policeman not only experiences a void in his existence but also finds his work least rewarding. He found that the police have more or less lost faith in themselves. They have not been able to develop any pride in their work and profession. In a way, they have been reduced to the state of merconaries whose only objective of existence is self-preservation and the monthly pay packets. Most policemen were found to suffer from a sense of frustration. They develop an indifference to their work which is reflected in the stagnation results in every sphere of their development, professional as well as ethical (Misra, 1972: xi).

Here it is highly important to note the observation made by Joseph Lehmen about the police officer as the symbol of the impartial authority of society while Ahmad, former DIG of Police of UP, has concluded his study on police in a welfare state that "the only way to control crime is to secure public co-operation" (Ahmad, 1957: 82).

Nettler Gwymn has found from his work on industrial societies that the rate of crime may vary with respect to rural urban areas and industrial and non-industrial areas. As observed by Nettler in industrialized societies, in recent times crime rates and prosperity seem to go together. Prosperity elevates crime statistics, it is said, because affluence is associated with better recording of offences (Gwymn, 1974:118).

Venugopal in his work *Facts of Crime in India* found that the distrust of the police is so heavily ingrained in the general police that the first inclination of the normal citizen is to keep away from the policeman as far as possible. The unfortunate impression even in educated and enlightened circles is that the police arc unscrupulous, ignorant, uncultured and corrupt and petty tyrants who prosecute the innocent and have little respect for individual liberty (Venugopal 1962: 183). P.D. Sharma in his study *Police Polity and People in India* arrived at the finding that "the lag between aspirations of people and their expectations of police performance is so wide that it is rather difficult even for the best friends of police to envisage a citizen police philosophy for Indian society in any foreseeable future" (Sharma, 1981:63).

Bhardwaj quotes from his work on police administration that the "objective of a public relations work is to make the people understand the nature of the police functions and majority of the people should extend co-operation and support to the police department." The goals of public relations as described by Bhardwaj are the following :

(a) *Public understanding* : There is primarily an educational goal which presupposes that an informed citizen is basic to effective law enforcement.

(b) *Public confidence* : There is mainly a psychological goal which involves the building of a citizen's trust and respect for the police and the department.

(c) *Public support* : This may take many forms such as compliance with the law, assistance in police investigations, and backing of measures to improve police service (Bhardwaj, 1978: 35-6).

S.K. Ghosh found in his work *Police in Ferment* that efficiency and high morale of the police cannot be achieved in reality only by the policemen. If there is any danger, it is not from the police but from politicians who either for personal or party interest, or from ignorance or malice might tidy up the apparent muddle of the many forces and organizations (Ghosh, 1981:127). P.D. Sharma in his study on police polity also found that as a crime prevention agency the usual charges levelled by the community against the police are : (1) The police is inefficient, inadequate and ill-trained for the job entrusted to it by the community; (2) it employs third-degree methods and is barbarous in its professional behaviour with the citizens; (3) it is corrupt and shares the booty with the criminals whom it seeks to detect and arrest (Sharma, 1981: 175). But Radzinowicz and Wolfgang found from their analysis on crime and justice that the police administration faces a problem in controlling practice with clients that is not found in most other organizations. The problem is that police are in contact with citizens in the community in such a manner that direct supervision is not possible (Radzinowicz and Wolfgang, 1971 : 161). However Venugopal Rao has found through his study of police service that in all these circumstances the police system has remained static in a rapidly changing society because the politician needed and used it for his narrow political ends and was not prepared to pay the price for an enlightened service (Rao, 1980:20).

S.K. Ghosh has revealed in his study *Police in Ferment* that the responses shown by different levels of police officialdom to these problems are varied and vivid. The senior police officers are, by and large, unwilling to deal swiftly and effectively with the wrongdoers within the force. So long as this remains the case not only will the public have no confidence in the police but policemen will also be encouraged to misbehave with citizens and harass them in various ways (Ghosh, 1981 : 41). Rammohan from his study on the image of the police in a changing society has concluded that the situation is more critical especially when the historical hangovers and the stereotype image of police organization in India are such that any enthusiasm for the implementation of law or public policy leaves an abuse of tools and an adverse impact upon the people who tend to view the police as an old enemy rather than a new friend (Rammohan, 1973: 13-18). Studies of Radelet on the minority group image in the work on police community has shown that young people are generally more negative than older persons in their attitudes towards the police. Similarly the poor generally have a less favourable attitude towards the police than the affluent (Radelet, 1977 : 134).

Peter K. Manning in his enquiry on police lying found that the issue of corruption was closely related to that of falsification or distortion of facts (Manning, 1974: 301-2).

From the findings of the study of the National Police Academy (1966) it was found that in the absence of social sanction against corruption in India legal section becomes too weak to be effective. P.D. Sharma specifically found in his study mentioned earlier that it was not always palatable to an honest senior to punish a corrupt junior of his own tribe when both of them shared the prevalent and dominant norms of their professional culture. He further revealed that several studies had pointed out that the state of corruption in the police ranks even at the lower levels was in no way worse than that in several other departments dealing with administration of revenue and economic affairs (Sharma, 1981:60-1).

Some studies of economic conditions and crime show a

correlation between periods of economic stress and higher crime rates. But Daniel Glezer and Kent Rice have challenged this finding that economic factors are probably a significant determinent of crime through their studies (Glazer and Rice, 1959 : 679-86).

Upendra Varma from his study on S.H.O. and the Indian police showed that police stations in urban areas were so much overworked with all sorts of quasi-police duties that they could not devote any special or even reasonable attention to offences committed against the members of weaker sections. Even if they desired to do, so, they got a very low priority (Varma, 1976 : 81-4).

Sharma observed as a conclusion from his work on police and community that professional frustrations, bordering on cynicism, weakened the moral fiber and it was bound to create a more serious kind of psychological void in the lives of those who lived in the midst of crime and criminals (Sharma, 1974 : 1-7).

Crime and Police in Kerala

"The concept of crime is rooted in man's rudimentary attempts to distinguish between right and wrong in his interaction with fellow humans" (Rao, 1981: 1). The criminal and the act of crime originate from the society under certain conditions of social process. Though various theories—ecological, individualistic or traditional—explain the phenomenon in different ways, the role of tradition and heritage in this regard cannot be ruled out. This is particularly relevant to the context of our society which is rooted in a strong tradition. References to theft, roberry, cheating, gambling, etc. as pastimes of kings in the *Rigveda* and other references to murder, adultery, inceat, etc. made by *Satapata Brahman* point to the instances of deviant behaviour as accepted practices in certain sections of the society in India. But *Manu Smriti* classified some offences as injurious and punishable by the State. References to Dharma and the principle of Karma in ancient Indian literature as the self-regulating principles for the individual though the prescription of physical or mental punishment, are an important aspect in the Indian attitude towards crime and its treatment. In the context of changing attitude towards life and customs, the criminal justice system accepts new channels of procedure. The emergence of Indian Penal Code and the provisions for classifying offences have clearly differentiated the cognizable and non-cognizable offences. The concept of right and wrong assumed new diamensions particularly based on a legal, rational and social point of view.

In Kerala crime statistics have shown distinct features with respect to cognizable offences.

Table 1.1

Crime Conditions relating to all Cognizable Cases reported under IPC and Special and Local Laws (1969-79) in Kerala

Year	*No. of Cases*	*Variation*	*Percentage of Variation*
1969	33405	+ 864	2.7
1970	35166	+1761	5.3
1971	33052	—2114	6.0
1972	37467	+4415	13.4
1973	44163	+6696	17.9
1974	46120	+1957	4.4
1975	41268	—4852	10.5
1976	35118	—6150	14.9
1977	43481	+8363	23.8
1978	52309	+8828	20.3
1979	46672	—5637	10.8

Source : Government of Kerala, *Administration Report of the Police Department*, 1979.

It may be found from the above distribution that crime rate was continuing an increasing trend every year till 1975, and it continued except during 1976 and 1979. This change may particularly be due to the improved law and order situation and the political stability of the state during the above period. This could be achieved mainly because of the proclamation of national emergency during 1975-6 and its role in reducing the crime rate may have been quite significant. In Kerala, the year 1979 was specially noted for achieving a moderate social order by the police from the viewpoint of reported offences and calamities. Though the political situation in Kerala during 1979 was not perfectly stable at the top level, the conflict in the different political units had not spread among the masses resorting to political violences or attrocities as in the case of few of the former years. This fact may also be due to the conscious preparation of the political parties and leaders to face the by-elections at Kasargode, Tellicherry, Thiruvalla and Parassala Assembly Constituencies and the approaching general election in 1980.

An important feature of the crime situation in Kerala observed from different sources is the predominance of cases of hurt, rioting theft, rash actions endangering the life of individuals, lurking and house-breaking. In 1979 there were 11,083 hurt cases, 4,468 instances of rioting, 3,342 reports of theft, 3,521 reports of rash action, and 3,586 reports of lurking and house-breaking in the state. It may also be added that among these reports on hurt cases and those on rash actions were showing an increase over the previous year and others manifested a negative variation.

With regard to the crime investigation and detection the police in Kerala have shown remarkable interest and effort in completing investigation and presenting cases.

The police organization in the state is one of the efficient service departments of state machinery. The law and order situation in the state has been well-guarded by the Kerala police in spite of the precedental political instability and problems to which the society had been exposed. On all these occasions of conflicting ideologies in authority of the state machinery, the Kerala police had recorded its efficiency and loyalty to the state discipline. Though the police association has emerged as a new development in the system it has not affected any of the policies' and programmes of the police force in Kerala.

The police department in Kerala functions under the Home department and currently is under the supreme command of the Director General and Inspector General of Police. The major organizational divisions of the police system constitute Intelligence, Administration (H.Q.), Law and Order, and Crimes. Each of these has been assigned to the overall responsibility of one Inspector General of Police. As per the latest arrangement, the Inspector General of law and order is also holding the charge

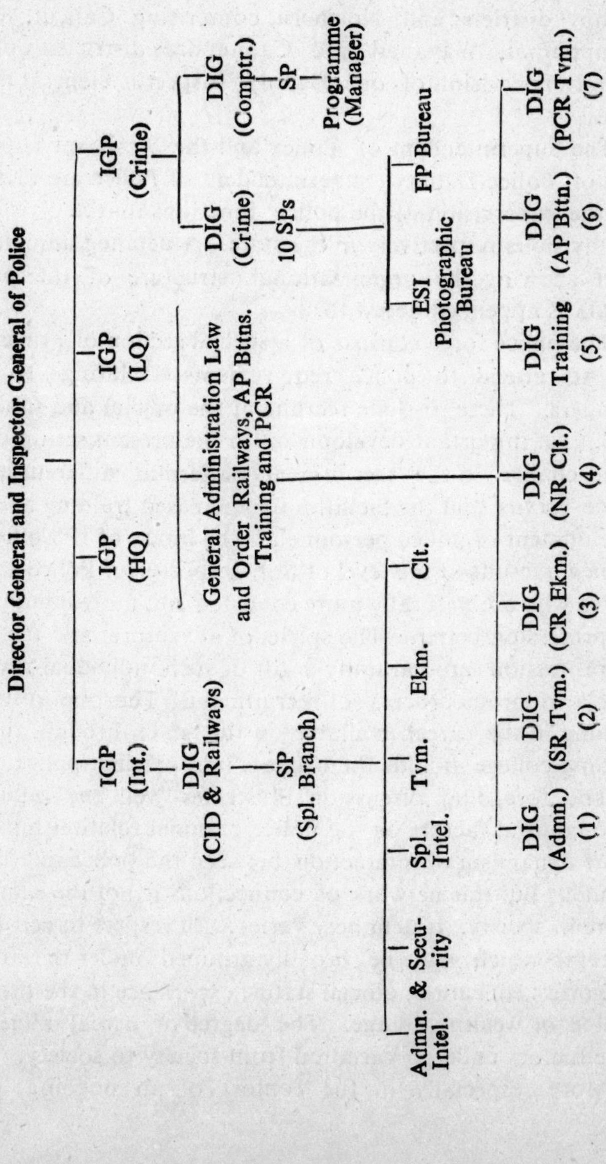

Director General and Inspector General of Police
IGP (Int.)
IGP (HQ)
IGP (LQ)
IGP (Crime)
DIG (CID & Railways)
SP (Spl. Branch)
Admn. & Intel.
Security
Spl. Intel.
Tvm.
Ekm.
Clt.
General Administration Law and Order Railways, AP Bttns. Training and PCR
DIG (Crime)
10 SPs
ESI Photographic Bureau
FP Bureau
DIG (Comptr.)
SP
Programme (Manager)
DIG (Admn.) (1)
DIG (SR Tvm.) (2)
DIG (CR Ekm.) (3)
DIG (NR Clt.) (4)
DIG Training (5)
DIG (AP Bttn.) (6)
DIG (PCR Tvm.) (7)

of general administration at Headquarter (Trivandrum). The police organization outside the Headquarter has been divided into three major regions, namely Southern, comprising Trivandrum, Quilon, Pathanamthitta and Alleppey districts; Central, consisting of Ernakulam, Kottayam, Idukki and Trichur districts; and Northern, comprising Calicut, Palghat, Malappuram, Wayanad and Cannanore districts, under the overall supervision of one Deputy Inspector General of Police each.

The Superintendent of Police and the Assistant Superintendent of Police/Deputy Superintendent of Police are responsible for the supervision of the police functions in the divisions and sub-divisions respectively in the state. A detailed administrative chart showing the organizational structure of the police in Kerala is appended herewith.

The police force consists of a special section of women police also to attend to police requirements relating to women offenders. These include recruits at the official and subordinate level. An important development in the present set-up of police is the change in the recruitment pattern at different levels of police service and the facilities for increased training and career development of police personnel. The influx of IPS officers and the new recruits at the level of Sub-Inspector of Police and other cadres who are naturally more educated and more equipped suits the profession better. The spirits of adventure and the skill for the profession are naturally a gift of such individual who come after a rigorous process of recruitment. The opportunities for training in the career available in the state through the police training college moulds the trainees into efficient policemen.

The foregoing discussion illustrates well the influence of socio-cultural factors on the police-criminal relationships as well as the dynamism of interaction between the police and the community. But this network of connections is not the same everywhere in society. It definitely varies with respect to certain valid concepts which may be broadly grouped under the following categories: education, official status, experience in the profession, income or wealth and age. The degree of actual influences of these factors undergo variation from society to society.

More especially in the context of an ongoing political

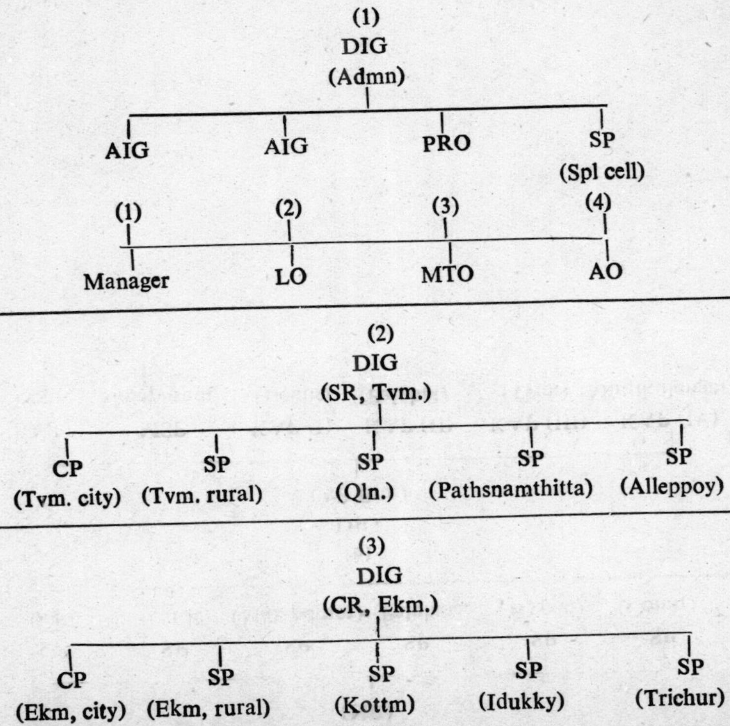
(1)
DIG
(Admn)
AIG
AIG
PRO
SP
(Spl cell)
(1)
(2)
(3)
(4)
Manager
LO
MTO
AO
(2)
DIG
(SR, Tvm.)
CP
(Tvm. city)
SP
(Tvm. rural)
SP
(Qln.)
SP
(Pathsnamthitta)
SP
(Alleppoy)
(3)
DIG
(CR, Ekm.)
CP
(Ekm, city)
SP
(Ekm, rural)
SP
(Kottm)
SP
(Idukky)
SP
(Trichur)

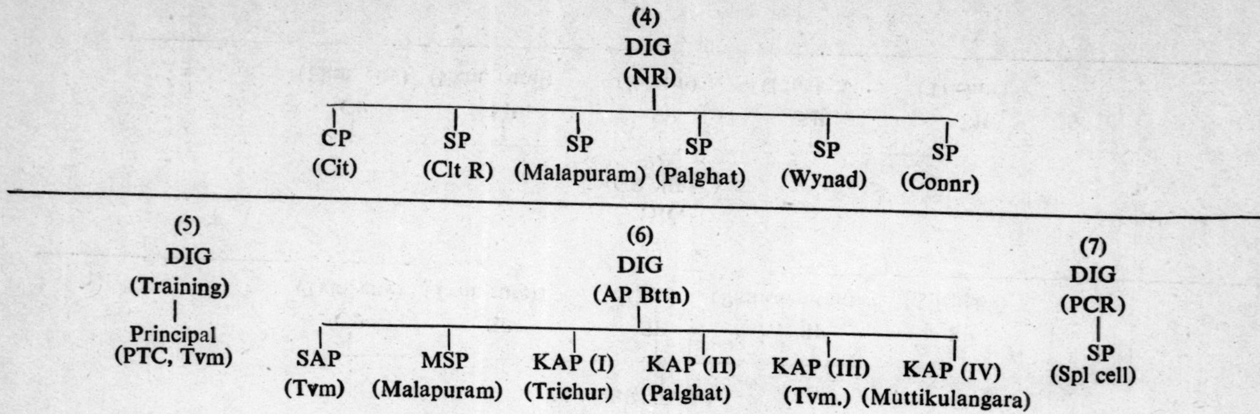
(4)
DIG
(NR)
CP
(Cit)
SP
(Clt R)
SP
(Malapuram)
SP
(Palghat)
SP
(Wynad)
SP
(Connr)
(5)
DIG
(Training)
Principal
(PTC, Tvm)
(6)
DIG
(AP Bttn)
SAP
(Tvm)
MSP
(Malapuram)
KAP (I)
(Trichur)
KAP (II)
(Palghat)
KAP (III)
(Tvm.)
KAP (IV)
(Muttikulangara)
(7)
DIG
(PCR)
SP
(Spl cell)

District Level Administration

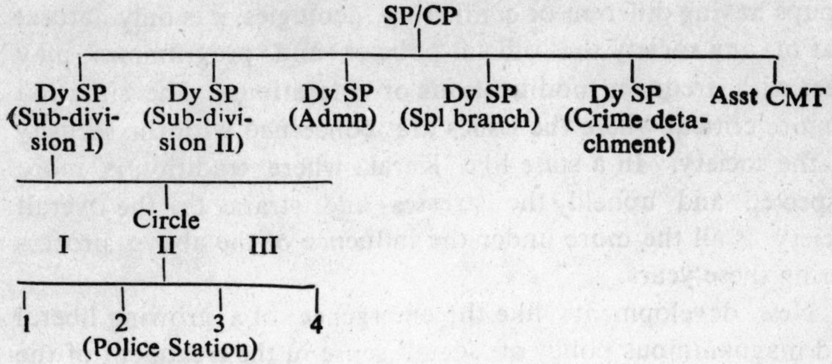

Note :

IGP —Inspector General of Police
DIG —Deputy Inspector General of Police
SP —Superintendent of Police
CP —Commissioner of Police
AIG —Assistant Inspector General of Police
Dy SP —Deputy Superintendent of Police
ASP —Assistant Superintendent of Police

Int. —Intelligence
HQ —Headquarters
Admn —Administration
PCR —Protection of Civil Rights
SR —Southern Range
CR —Central Range
NR —Northern Range
Comptr —Computer
Bttn —Battalion

Tvm —Trivandrum
Qln —Quilon
Kottm —Kottayam
Ekm —Ernakulam

SAP —Special Armed Police
MSP —Malabar Special Police
KAP —Kerala Armed Police
PTC —Police Training College

instability characterized by the assuming of power by different groups having different or conflicting ideologies, it is only natural that in any society the official policies and programmes may meet with frequent modifications or alterations. The situation is more critical where the issues are concerned with the security of the society. In a state like Kerala where tradition is more respected and upheld the stresses and strains on the overall society is all the more under the influence of the above process during these years.

New developments like the emergence of a growing liberal and magnanimous policy of 'social' sense in the treatment of the offender, the law breaker, police association, the growing political involvements in these and the nature and extent of commitment of the police, etc. are issues of great concern today. These factors when viewed from the angle of changing police-criminal as well as police-community relations necessitates a new kind of approach. It was hence decided to enquire into the details of the various phenomena related to the problem. It is hoped that these enquiries will not only throw light on the real pattern of interactions, but also the outcome, as felt or experienced by the three entities, namely the criminal, the poilce and the community. In the following pages this enquiry is elaborated and emperically verified.

2

METHODOLOGY

In every society criminal behaviour on the one hand and police behaviour on the other, assume various dimensions of interactive patterns. In such situations, the community around both functions as a silent spectator. Today the deviant and the disciplinarian or the police are more alert towards social problems. Under this set-up a new process of relationship between the police, the offender and the community develops in society. The nature of these relationships depends more on the existing social structure. In order to understand more about the details of these relationships it would be highly necessary to view the problem from a more sophisticated angle.

The Research Problem

The objective of this study is mainly to investigate into the manifested existing relationship between the police, the offenders or criminals and the community around through their outward behaviour in different social situations. The police-offender relationship under the influence of community interaction in the local set-up constitutes the subject matter of the study. This study on criminal behaviour and the police in the community proposes to concentrate on the positive and negative types of contributions emerging out of the interaction process that is evident in modern Kerala. Thus, in the present study we have attempted to bring out in detail the extent to which the above process of interaction has been manifested and what are their implications in Kerala society today.

Hypotheses

1. The major hypotheses in this programme may be worded as follows. The nature of police behaviour towards criminals is very much related to the social and individual anticidents of the offender. The educational background of the offender and the nature of police behaviour are related. The official status of the police and the police behaviour towards the offender are related. Superior rank holders in police are more considerate in behaviour towards more educated offenders in the community.
2. In modern society, the nature of police behaviour depends more on the income status of the offender. Top officials and officials among police are generally more considerate towards offenders from higher income groups.
3. Professional experience of police personnel and their behaviour towards offenders are related. Police officers of relatively higher standing or experience in the profession tend to be more considerate or less cruel towards offenders in modern society. Aging in police and the nature of their relationship to the offenders are interconnected. The more aged the officer, the more considerate he is towards offenders.
4. Among police personnel, official status of individuals and prevalence of corruption among them are related. Police personnel with longer service in the profession tend to be corrupt.
5. Official status of the police influences seriously the nature of police-community relations. Officials and top officials in police service tend to be more capable of maintaining smooth relations with the community.

Definition of Concepts

Criminal behaviour : For the purpose of this study, the

erm 'criminal behaviour' may mean that type of behaviour expressed by an individual by an act which is forbidden by the existing law and injurious to the person himself who commits it and to others who are the victims or sufferers of the social action. The manifestation of criminal behaviour may be vivid and varied.

Crime : Crime refers to an action or series of actions punishable under the provisions of the Indian Penal Code.

Police : The term for the purpose of this study refers to hat branch of the police force which is engaged in the general xecutive police functions in the state, namely the local police.

Offender : Offender or criminal in this study may mean any dult male or female individual who violates the law and is eing kept under judicial custody for reasons charged against im/her.

Top officials : For the purpose of this study, the term 'top fficials' may mean those police officers who are in the rank of y. SP/ASP and above.

Officials : The term 'officials' in this study refers to police fficials in the Kerala State Police Service, who are holding ositions ranging from Assistant Sub-Inspector to that of Circle ıspector of Police.

Subordinate officials : In this study, the term 'subordinate fficials' may refer to individuals in the cadres of Constables nd Head Constables in the police service.

Community : "Community as a term conveys the idea of a t of people who have many things in common. It is a group hich shares ideas, beliefs, customs and norms" (Hubert, 1968 : 1). In this study we mean the term to apply to the social unit the immediate vicinity within a radius of two to three kilo- etres around a particular police unit, namely the police station.

Police brutality : Police brutality, in the context of the esent study, primarily refers to a type of police behaviour wards the offenders especially during interrogation. Use of usive language, physical assault, threatening of several kinds, ychological projections on offenders, etc. are some of the mmon manifested features reported in this connection.

Third-degree methods : The term for the purpose of this udy means an aspect of police behaviour and forms a part of the act of police brutality. It refers to the rigorous methods adopted by the police resorting mainly to severe physical assault towards the offenders during the process of crime investigation.

Discriminatory treatment : In this study, discriminatory treatment may refer to that type of dealing which the police adopts towards offenders with a clear sense of partiality. Difference in degree and intensity in the inflictment of third-degree methods, the conditions of police brutality, shouting or adopting certain special concessions to some of the offenders, etc. are some of the examples. Very commonly instances of such partialities are on the basis of differences in income, educational status and other social distinctions that we may have.

Professionalism : For the purpose of our analysis, the term refers to the extent of mastery and efficiency developed by the police in executing the police functions. The degree of attainment of this quality of the officers is a major aspect of police career in public service.

Non-individual factors : By this term we intend to indicate all the factors appearing in the process of police, criminal-community relations which are not at all related to the subjective conditions of either of these categories.

Locality : In this study, we mean locality to represent the geographical location or boundaries of groups or communities included in the study.

Corruption : Corruption for the purpose of this study mean corrupt practices of any form adopted by the police while discharging official duties. This may include instances of dereliction of one's duty on the part of police, acceptance of bribes or similar benefits, subjecting oneself to extraordinary external influences at the cost of social justice for the common man, etc

Population and Sample

The population for the study consists of offenders or criminals under judicial custody, police officials of different rank in state service and members of the community around police stations in Kerala. Among the different branches of police force in the state, the general police or local police constitute the population for the study. The distribution showing th

Table 2.1
Strength of Local Police as on March 1982 in the State of Kerala

Sl. No.	District	CP/SP	ACP/ASP Dy SP	CIs	SIs	ASIs	HCs	PCs	Population (1981)*
1.	Trivandrum (city and rural)	2	9	18	78	38	343	1312	2591057
2.	Quilon	1	4	12	45	28	181	646	2807223
3.	Alleppey	1	4	11	42	26	171	714	2342852
4.	Kottayam	1	4	9	34	23	160	571	1681104
5.	Idukki	1	5	11	33	24	145	625	971193
6.	Eranakulam (city and rural)	2	10	21	72	35	287	1179	2533265
7.	Trichur	1	4	11	39	27	146	542	2436975
8	Malappuram	1	4	10	35	25	165	594	2401229
9.	Palghat	1	4	10	39	26	163	769	2041912
10.	Calicut (city aad rural)	2	7	16	55	27	259	1117	2796352
11.	Cannanore	1	5	13	61	39	240	1130	2800055
	Total	14	60	142	533	318	2260	9199	25403217

Source : Official records of the Police Department, Government of Kerala, Trivandrum, 1981-2.

*Census of India, 1981.

**Including Waynad District also.

CP—Commissioner of Police; SP—Superintendent of Police; ACP—Assistant Commissioner of Police; ASP—Assistant Superintendent of Police; CI—Civil Inspector; SI—Sub-Inspector; HC—Head Constable.

details of the strength of police in Kerala as per the latest available data is given in table 2.1.

As the above action of the police, namely the Local police was actually in close interaction with the society and its problems, it was thought to limit the study to this section of the police to have a fuller and more realistic understanding of police-offender relationship under the influence of a given society.

The major sampling method resorted to in this study was systematic sampling. For the purpose of sampling, three major zones i.e. north, central and south of the police administration were taken into consideration. Based on actual reported crimes in the districts during 1979, two districts each from the three zones were selected. They were selected in such a way so as to have one of these two districts having the highest reported crime rate and the other one where the Regional Headquarter was located. Thus Cannanore and Calicut districts from Northern zone, Ernakulam and Kottayam Districts from Central zone; and Quilon and Trivandrum from South zone were selected. There was a total of 186 police stations in these six districts. A fifty per cent sample of these 186 stations were selected for the study. Thus, altogether from the six districts mentioned above, 83 police stations were to be covered for data collection. These police stations were selected on the basis of reported cases (1979). During sample selection, from each police station giving due representation to police hierarchy, items were selected so as to have one each from the official level and three items each from the subordinate level. Regarding the inclusion of higher officials or top officials in the sample it is needless to say that all the higher officials were included in the sample. Thus, altogether the sample size came to 372 for the police. As 9 officials at the district or sub-divisional headquarter and 13 other respondents at the respective police stations were not available or had other excuses like unavoidable urgent official work and other engagements, these items could not be covered while data collection. Thus, the sample size in this section had to be limited to 350. We took relatively a large sample so as to have maximum representation in the sample.

The sample of offenders was taken from those originally charged from the police stations in the selected area and kept

Table 2.2

Details of Cognizable Offences Reported under IPC during the year 1979 in the Districts

Name of District	*No. of Cases of Offences*
Trivandrum	6055
Quilon	4052
Alleppey	3892
Kottayam	2857
Idukki	1716
Ernakulam	5044
Trichur	2818
Palghat	2655
Malappuram	1956
Kozhikode	2760
Cannanore	3161
Total	36966

Source : Official records of the Police Department, Government of Kerala, Trivandrum, 1980.

under judicial custody in the Central Jail Cannanore, Sub Jail Cannanore, District Jail Calicut, Sub Jail Ernakulam, Sub Jail Quilon, Sub Jail Trivandrum and Central Prison Trivandrum, which fall in the jurisdiction of the original districts selected for data collection during the period of study. The sample items in this regard were selected at the rate of five cases for every selected police station for the study. Thus, the whole sample came to 415. But during data collection, all the 415 items could not be covered mainly due to official and technical objection for not making available the actual offenders for data collection. Such respondents of non-availability came to 85 in number. Thus, the effective sample size in this item was to be limited to 330 for the study.

In the case of selecting sample items from the community members in order to have a sufficiently representative group in the aggregate, the principle of selecting three adult members at random from the immediate vicinity within a radius of two kilometres from the concerned police station was followed based on the latest voters list available in the respective areas. The total number of such items was worked out to 249 for the whole study. During fieldwork some of the sample items could not be traced due to incomplete addresses, looking outs, change of residence, etc. In such cases nearly items were substituted. There were 11 such cases. Even on repeated consecutive callings, some of the respondents could not be obtained for data collection. Some of the members originally agreed and fixed appointments for data collection were hesitant to give information at the time of interview on questions in the area of study. There were 7 such missing cases in this category. In a few other cases, complete information could not be obtained and hence they had to be deleted from our list. Taking into consideration all these cases and rectifying the possible defects, it needs to be pointed out that from a total of 29 cases, we could get no complete worthy information and as such they had to be discarded from the original list. Hence, the sample size in this part ultimately came to 220.

Pilot Study

A pre-test was conducted initially in the three different zones for obtaining a preliminary idea of the data on the basis of a comprehensive interview guide prepared for the purpose. Based on the observation of the pilot study, the final schedule was formulated to make an effective research tool for data collection.

Data Collection

The data collection in this study was complete in three phases, i.e. collection of the theoretical materials, collection of documentary evidences and other secondary data from official and other sources available. A major part of the study depended on primary data collected through fieldwork. The data was supplemented by extensive field notes obtained from other relevant sources also.

Tools of Data Collection

The main tools of data collection adopted for the study were personal interview, interview schedules, formal and informal discussions on relevant issues with officials and other members related to the study.

Fieldwork was conducted during 1980-81. The offenders were interviewed at the jails concerned. The police officials were interviewed in their offices and police stations and community members at their respective residences. Some were interviewed in the police stations too.

Independent Variables

Major independent variables fixed for the study included education of police, criminals and community members, official status and length of service of the police, age of police and offenders, and the history of punishment of offenders.

We have adopted the classification for education as illiterate, primary, upper primary, high school and above for offenders and below SSLC, college-educated, graduation and above for police and community members.

Official status was classified into subordinates, officials and top officials. Major age groups selected for the study were : below 20 years; 20 to 30 years; 30 to 40 years; 40 to 50 years; and 50 years and above.

Dependent Variables

They were mainly police behaviour, nature of response to reported cases, disposal of cases, mode of relationship between police and community members, police corruption, etc.

Analysis of Data

Data was analysed on the basis of the relationship between the selected independent variables and other dependent variables relevant to the problem. The data was codified, classified and tabulated in the prescribed manner to facilitate the means of analysis. Statistical tests applied for the analysis of the data were Chi-square test and Pearson's Coefficient of Association.

Chi-square test was calculated with the help of the formula $X^2=\frac{(f_o-f_e)^2}{f_e}$ where X^2 refers to the value of Chi-square, f_o to observed frequency of the sub-classes, and f_e to the expected frequency of the sub-class. The degree of freedom (DF) in the distribution was estimated following the rule that DF=(N−1) (n−1) where N stands for the number of rows and n for the number of columns in the table.

Pearson's Coefficient of Association was applied to examine the degree of association in the relationship of the variables. Pearson's coefficient of mean square contingency was worked out on the basis of the derivation that $P=\sqrt{\frac{x^2}{x^2+8}}$ where P stands for coefficient of association and s for the sample size. The value of the coefficient normally remained within the range of 0 to 1; the value nearing I may be taken to be indicative of the existence of a strong association between the variables and vic versa.

3

POLICE BEHAVIOUR

Convergence of existing social norms and social justice is important in every society. Implementation of these normative prescriptions depends exclusively on the responsibility of the law enforcing body, commonly the police. The preconditions to police service or even the very function of the police in relation to crime treatment are not the same everywhere. They assume different patterns depending on the situation. Although the primary police purpose is to deal with criminals in action, the bulk of daily transactions is related to the secondary purposes of crime prevention and a wide variety of regulatory functions not concerned directly with criminals (Johnson, 1968 : 366). In this context, the relationships within the criminal justice system—between police and prosecutor, between police and courts, between prosecutor and courts, between police and corrections, between courts and corrections—are highly important. (Radelet, 1977 : 319).

In a free society, the effectiveness of the police force largely depends on its acceptability to law abiding citizens (Mark, 1972: 66). Such groups give more weight to the behaviour of the police towards the community in their dealings. The police generally adopt varying methods, simple or tough, in dealing with investigation of offences. Though it is very common in the behaviour of the police even in modern society, the use of third-degree methods in eliciting information or confessions from the accused or suspects is considered as a malpractice in law enforcement (Bhardwaj, 1978 : 312). By way of behavioural variations among police personnel, Chaturvedi has pointed out complaints against police as ranging from instances of cruelty and indifference to duty, to dishonest investigation, illegal detention, collusion with criminals, rudeness towards people and even corruption and practice of third-degree methods (Chaturvedi, 1980 : 1).

It is also quite common that often the police employ lawless methods (including the third-degree) or prolonged or brutal interviews, make false arrests, including arrests on suspicion and tap wires to secure evidence (Elliot and Morrill, 1961 : 555). Policemen often confess to the use of third-degree methods against suspects in police custody but their arguments is that any method that deals with hard criminals cannot be first degree (Sharma, 1980 : 70). Thus, for the police it is an art and a fine art to handle a criminal sympathetically and properly. But in many cases the causes are : (1) unsympathetic and cruel treatment to a man by the police, (2) economic distress and (3) lack of facility to find healthy employment and peaceful vocation (Ahmad, 1957 : 76). It is under these circumstances that Badelet gives three levels of definitions to police brutality. One of the meanings of brutality is its literal interpretation, the use of undue or unreasonable physical force in some aspects of police action. Another level of definition is verbal or psychological brutality. The police officer as a symbol of the system is brutal because the system brutalizes (Radelet, 1973 : 210).

Following these arguments, it may be pointed out that several factors are associated with police behaviour, and the important of them are social, economic and individualistic or personal. These are found to be operating on both the police force and the victims involved in the problem. Very often the manifestations of these behaviours are through the educational, communal, economic and even temperamental characters of the members involved.

Accordingly in this chapter, it is intended to analyse the relationship between the nature of police behaviour towards the offenders or criminals and the socio-personal background of the criminals. We propose to measure these in terms of age, education, income and the history of punishment of the criminals.

Behaviourism of Police

Our hypothesis in this regard is that educational, income or other similar social factors strongly influence the manifestations of police behaviour towards criminals. More educated criminals experience relatively more tolerable behaviour from police. Criminals with a longer history of punishment experience more intolerable behaviour from police. Previous prejudice among police as an important factor here. Here the feelings of the criminals about the actual spirit of the police in their dealings with crime situations were studied. It was seen from the analysis (Table 3.1) that the majority (72.1%) of offenders had experienced the police treatment towards them as quite intolerable. In order

Table 3.1

Police Behaviour and the Educational Level of Offenders

Police Behaviour	*Educational Level of Offenders*				*Total*
	Illiterate	*Primary*	*Upper Primary*	*High School and Above*	
Cordial and co-operative	12 (16.7%)	32 (22.1%)	17 (26.2%)	11 (22.9%)	72 (21.8%)
Tolerable	4 (5.6%)	7 (4.8%)	5 (7.1%)	2 (4.2%)	18 (5.5%)
Intolerable	56 (77.7%)	106 (73.1%)	43 (66.1%)	35 (72.9%)	240 (72.7%)
Total	72 (100%)	145 (100%)	65 (100%)	48 (100%)	330 (100%)

Chi-square value=2.97; DF=6

Table value at .05 level of significance=12.59.

to test whether the educational background of the offenders had any influence on such experiences the data were examined in detail and it was found that as many as 72.9 per cent of the respondents who had an educational background of high school and above maintained the view that police behaviour was not tolerable towards them. Here it was specially found that only a few (22.9%) of the group could find a cordial co-operative kind of behaviour from the police.

Among the illiterate respondents too, the majority (77.7%) of respondents found police interaction intolerable. This observation holds good more or less in a similar condition for other educational categories as well as can be seen very clearly from Table 3.1. Hence it is to be inferred that police behaviour towards criminals is independent of educational background or equipment of criminals. The chi-square test showed that there was no significant relationship between the level of education of criminals and police behaviour.

In ordinary situations law breakers may not be having similar experiences from law enforcing bodies. This depends predominantly on the nature of the enforce and the enforced in many respects. In the context of the present study also, the police under the influence of the executive authority vested in it and the offenders as the enforced are no exception to this. Some of the important conditions which are influential factors in police behaviour towards offenders are age, income background and the history of punishment of the criminal concerned.

Hence, taking into consideration the importance of these factors, it was thought to examine the data on police behaviour towards offenders with respect to the age of the respondents. As revealed in Table 3.2, it was found that the majority (154 out of 240, i.e. 64.1%) of those offenders who had experienced police behaviour as intolerable were in the age group of twenty to thirty years. On a detailed analysis of the data with respect to the age of the respondents also, it was found that 89.6 per cent of the criminals who were in the age group of twenty to thirty years had the same experience. It has been interestingly found in the analysis that relatively more aged offenders were few (22.7%) in the sample as indicated by the percentages having this kind of experience. Incidentally it may be pointed out here that the majority (72.7%) of the offenders who were aged above fifty years admitted that the police was cordial and co-operative towards them in behaviour. The data in this part of the analysis showed that police behaviour was more critical towards

Table 3.2

Police Behaviour and Age of the Offenders

Police Behaviour	*Age of Offenders*					*Total*
	Below 20 years	*20-30 years*	*30-40 years*	*40-50 years*	*Above 50 years*	
Co-operative and cordial	6 (20.7%)	9 (5.2%)	24 (35.8%)	17 (42.5%)	16 (72.7%)	72 (21.8%)
Tolerable	4 (13.8%)	9 (5.2%)	3 (4.5%)	1 (2.5%)	1 (4.6%)	18 (5.5%)
Intolerable	19 (65.5%)	154 (89.6%)	40 (59.7%)	22 (55.0%)	5 (22.7%)	240 (72.7%)
Total	29 (100%)	172 (100%)	67 (100%)	40 (100%)	22 (100%)	330 (100%)

youngsters, namely those who were in the age group of twenty to thirty years and it was more considerate towards old people. Table 3.2 was rearranged (Table 3.3) for applying the chi-square test. The chi-square test showed the relationship between the variables at 5% level of confidence. The value of Pearson's coefficient of association (0.40) also showed that there was moderately good association between the age of the offender and police behaviour.

Table 3.3

Police Behaviour and Age of the Offenders (Rearranged)

Police Behaviour	*Age of Offenders*					*Total*
	Below 20 years	*20-30 years*	*30-40 years*	*40-50 years*	*Above 50 years*	
Co-operative, cordial and tolerable	10	18	27	18	17	90
Intolerable	19	154	40	22	5	240
Total	29	172	67	40	22	330

Chi-square=65.03; DF=4

Table value at .05 level of significance=9.48

Pearson's coefficient of association=0.40

It is quite common that the reaction as well as the tolerance capacity of the offenders in this regard may well depend on one's standard of life and the general background of the social life he enjoys. On all these occasions one's income is an appropriate indication and even a determinant, to some extent, in developing attitudes towards others' behaviour to oneself. Hence, taking into consideration the income background of the offenders and the police behaviour towards them, the data were studied in details. It was found that a majority (74.5%) of the offenders in the sample belonged to the income group of Rs. 100 to Rs. 300 per month. On studing the data on police behaviour with respect to the income of the respondents, it was found that a large majority (82.5%) of the respondents belonging to the above income group had bad experience with the police. It may also be noted that among those offenders who felt that the police were intolerable, a considerably major section (84.5%) belonged to the lower income group of Rs. 100 to 300 per month. In this connection it may also be noted that 52 per cent of the offenders from the higher income group had enjoyed a cordial attitude in the treatment towards them from the police side. The chi-square test showed a significant relationship between the income of the offenders and the mode of police behaviour as experienced by

Table 3.4
Police Behaviour and Monthly Income of the Offenders

Police Behaviour	*Family Income (Rs)*			*Total*
	0-100	*100-300*	*300-500*	
Cordial and co-operative	21 (35.6%)	38 (15.5%)	13 (52.0%)	72 (21.8%)
Tolerable	7 (11.9%)	5 (2.0%)	6 (24.0%)	18 (5.5%)
Intolerable	31 (52.5%)	203 (82.5%)	6 (24.0%)	240 (72.7%)
Total	59 (100%)	246 (100%)	25 (100%)	330 (100%)

Chi-square=59.99; DF=4
Table value at .05 level of significance=9.49
Pearson's coefficient of association=0.39

the offenders. Details are shown in table 3.4. The value of Pearson's coefficient of association (0.39) also indicates moderate association between the variables.

In order to understand more about police-offender relations, an understanding of the outward manifestations of behaviour of the police towards criminals, especially the nature and type of physical torture when the offenders are in the custody of the police becomes essential. Accordingly on our enquiry, it was found from the study that there were only 40.9 per cent respondents who had not experienced any physical inflictments from the police during questioning. However, a majority (59.0%, i.e.,

195 out of 330) of the criminals in the sample have admitted to experiencing physical torture while in police custody. In these matters it is very likely that the police dealings with the offenders may vary according to the age of the offenders as the reaction from the police to different members and particularly certain age groups may not be similar always. Hence the data was re-examined with respect to the age of the offenders on the behaviour of the police. It was seen that among those who had admitted to experiencing severe physical torture majority (56.9%, i.e. 66 out of 116) came from the age group of twenty to thirty years. It can also be seen from Table 3.5 that among respondents from this age group, a majority (63.9%, i.e. 110 out of 172) admitted to experiencing casual beatings and other severe physical torture from police. This shows that brutality of police behaviour targetted at the offenders in this respect was more commonly suffered by people in the age group of 20-30 years. It can be seen in the analysis that among offenders belonging to the age group of fifty years and above in the sample, a majority (77.3%) have admitted to no experience of physical torture from the police. Likewise among respondents in the age group of below 20 years also the behaviour of the police was found to be a considerate one as 48.3 per cent respondents admitted to no experience of physical torture by them. It was specially observed that as the age of the offenders increased there was a gradual decrease of unkind behaviour by the police towards them. The chi-square test showed that there is a significant relationship between the two variables at .05 per cent level of confidence.

The Criminal and Police Bias

It has been often felt that the police behaviour towards offenders always depends on previous acquaintance with the police especially in relation to crime behaviour. Here the previous criminal history of the offenders and the nature of criminal career and the background of the offenders are significant points. These factors are very likely to instill prejudices or bias among the police towards offenders. Hence, it was a matter of interest to enquire into the nature of police behaviour towards such offenders in the study. Accordingly, we

Table 3.5

Experience of Physical Torture from the Police and the Age of Offenders

Experience of Physical Torture	*Age of Offenders*					*Total*
	Below 20 years	*20-30 years*	*30-40 years*	*40-50 years*	*Above 50 years*	
No experience of physical torture	14 (48.3%)	62 (36.1%)	28 (41.8%)	14 (35 0%)	17 (77.3%)	135 (40.9%)
Casual beating	8 (27.6%)	44 (25.5%)	16 (23.9%)	10 (25.0%)	1 (4.5%)	79 (23.9%)
Severe torture	7 (24.1%)	66 (38.4%)	23 (34.3%)	16 (40.0%)	4 (18.2%)	116 (35.2%)
Total	29 (100%)	172 (100%)	67 (100%)	40 (100%)	22 (100%)	330 (100%)

Chi-square=15.78; DF=8
Table value at .05 level of significance=15.51.

Table 3.6

Nature of Bias Maintained by the Police and the Age of the Offenders

<table>
<tr><th>Nature of Bias</th><th colspan="5">Age of the Offenders</th><th>Total</th></tr>
<tr><th></th><th>Below 20 years</th><th>20-30 years</th><th>30-40 years</th><th>40-50 years</th><th>Above 50 years</th><th></th></tr>
<tr><td>No bias</td><td>8
(27.6%)</td><td>46
(26.7%)</td><td>20
(29.9%)</td><td>10
(25.0 |)</td><td>7
(31.8 |)</td><td>91
(27.6 |)</td></tr>
<tr><td>Intentional benevolent approach (reformative)</td><td>15
(51.7 |)</td><td>30
(17.5 |)</td><td>11
(16.4 |)</td><td>8
(20.0 |)</td><td>5
(22.7 |)</td><td>69
(20.9 |)</td></tr>
<tr><td>Prejudicial approach</td><td>6
(20.7 |)</td><td>96
(55.8 |)</td><td>36
(53.7 |)</td><td>22
(55.0 |)</td><td>10
(45.5 |)</td><td>170
(51.5 |)</td></tr>
<tr><td>Total</td><td>29
(100 |)</td><td>172
(100 |)</td><td>67
(100 |)</td><td>40
(100 |)</td><td>22
(100 |)</td><td>330
(100 |)</td></tr>
</table>

examined the data and following from the analysis in Table 3.6, it was seen that a majority (51.5%) of the sample felt that the police had a clear prejudicial approach towards the offenders with a long history of punishment. It may be noted that on the whole only 27.6 per cent of the respondents had the feeling that the police maintained no bias in their dealings with the offenders. However, it was noted from a few (20.9%) of the offenders in the sample that the police had an intentionally reformative approach towards them. In this context it will be recalled that these evaluations or feelings made by the offenders may certainly differ with respect to the age of the respondents especially in the context of the earlier finding on the influence of age of the offenders on police behaviour. A majority (56.5%) of those respondents who had maintained the view that the police behaved with a prejudicial approach towards offenders were relatively young aged between twenty to thirty years. It is particularly noted that members belonging to other age groups do not show much variation in this attitude. It is interesting to note from Table 3.6 that a majority (51.7%) of the young offenders i.c. those who are under twenty years looked upon police treatment as a benevolent one.

In any social situation, economic status functions as an influencial factor. This is true in the case of the behaviour of the police towards others also. Hence we have examined the role of economic factors in our study and in close relation with our earlier finding, the attitude of the police towards offenders depends to a great extent on the income background too. Thus, in our analysis of the data with respect to the family income of the offenders, it was clear that among those who had experienced a prejudicial kind of behaviour from the police a, considerable majority (74.5%, i.e. 246 out of 330) belonged to the income group of Rs. 100-300 per month. It can also be seen from Table 3.7 that the majority (52.0%) of those in this level of income background, namely Rs. 100-300 per month also felt that police retained a prejudicial approach towards them in their outward behaviour. This observation was noted at large (54.3%) among the respondents from the lowest income group too in the sample. Among the total respondents who had the strong feeling that the police behaviour to them was quite prejudicial in nature a, good majority (75.3%, i.e. 128 out of 170) belonged to the middle income group. Hence at this level of analysis it is to be inferred that members in the middle income category (Rs. 100-300 p.m.) are more critical towards police-offender relations in their actual experience. Table 3.7 discusses the results in detail.

Table 3.7

Nature of Bias Maintained by the Police and Income of the Offenders

Nature of Bias	*Family Income (Rs)*			*Total*
	0-100 per month	*100-300 per month*	*300-500 per month*	
No bias	15 (25.4%)	69 (28.1%)	7 (28.0%)	91 (27.6%)
Intentional benevolent (reformative)	12 (20.3%)	49 (19.9%)	8 (32.0%)	69 (20.9%)
Prejudicial approach	32 (54.3%)	128 (52.0%)	10 (40.0%)	170 (51.5%)
Total	59 (100%)	246 (100%)	25 (100%)	330 (100%)

In the assessment of the real behaviour of the police, one's educational level plays a significant role as it is quite a significant factor in enabling the individual to make more appropriate judgement on any issue. Accordingly, on studying the influence of the level of education of offenders in formulating an opinion on the behaviour of the police towards them it was found that while as large as 77.1 per cent of the offenders possessing the highest educational achievements in the sample, namely high school and above, maintained the view that the police was prejudicial in its behaviour towards them, only 26.1 per cent of the illiterate respondents could feel so in the study.

An important observation on the present analysis as

revealed by Table 3.8 is that while the largest part (44.4%) of illiterates in the sample felt that police maintained no bias or prejudice towards them, only 10.4 per cent of the respondents belonging to the highest educational level, namely high school and above had this reading. It may be specially seen in the study that higher the level of education of respondents, higher was the response in favour of existence of a prejudicial treatment on the part of the police.

Real attitude of the police towards the offenders on any issue depends more on the knowledge about the previous conditions especially in the criminal career of the offender.

Table 3.8

Nature of Bias Maintained by Police and the Educational Background of the Offenders

Nature of bias	*Educational Level of Offenders*				*Total*
	Illiterate	*Primary*	*Upper Primary*	*High School and Above*	
No bias	32 (44.4%)	39 (26.9%)	15 (23.1%)	5 (10.4%)	91 (27.6%)
Intentional benevolent approach (Reformative)	14 (19.5%)	36 (24.8%)	13 (20.0%)	6 (12.5%)	69 (20.9%)
Prejudicial approach	26 (36.1%)	70 (48.3%)	37 (56.9%)	37 (77,1%)	170 (51.5%)
Total	72 (100%)	145 (100%)	65 (100%)	48 (100%)	330 (100%)

Under these circumstances the development of prejudicial attitude or any sort of bias in the police-offender relations may well depend on the history of punishment or the nature of previous acquaintance of the offender also. Hence a reanalysis of the data on the basis of the history of previous punishments to which the offender was exposed was made and it was particularly seen that the largest part of respondents from every category in the history of punishment in the sample invariably admitted to experiencing prejudicial behaviour from the police as illustrated in Table 3.9. On a detailed examination of the data it was found that while a good majority (80.0%) of those

Table 3.9

Nature of Bias Maintained by the Police and the History of Punishment of Offenders

Nature of bias	*History of Punishment*				*Total*
	No Previous Punishment	*Punished Once*	*Punished Twice*	*Punished Thrice or More*	
No bias	80 (34.9%)	7 (12.5%)	4 (20.0%)	—	91 (27.6%)
Intentional benevolent approach (reformative)	55 (24.0%)	5 (8.9%)	4 (20.0%)	5 (20.0%)	69 (20.9%)
Prejudicial approach	94 (41.1%)	44 (78.6%)	12 (60.0%)	20 (80.0%)	179 (51.5%)
Total	229 (100%)	56 (100%)	20 (100%)	25 (100%)	330 (100%)

who had a long history of punishment of thrice and more retained this view, only 41.1 per cent of the first offenders could feel so. A major part (60.0%) of those respondents who were convicted twice also had to come to similar conclusions from their experience after they were convicted. This analysis shows that police always retains a prejudicial way of approach towards the recidivists. It was specially observed in this study that this prejudicial behaviour increases with respect to the increase in the history of punishment of the offenders as detailed in Table 3.9. In order to apply the chi-square test the table was rearranged clubbing columns 4 and 5 so as to have the requirements of expected frequency of items in individual columns to enable the test as shown in Table 3.10.

Table 3.10

Nature of Bias Maintained by the Police as and the History of Punishment (Rearranged)

Nature of Bias	*History of Punishment*			*Total*
	No Previous Punishment	*Punished Once*	*Punished Twice or More*	
No bias	80	7	4	91
Intentional benevolent approach (reformative)	55	5	9	69
Prejudicial approach	94	44	32	170
Total	229	56	45	330

Chi-square=35.95; DF=4
Table value at .05 level of significance=9.42

The chi-square test showed that the relationship between the history of punishment of offenders and the nature of bias on the part of police are significant at .05 level of confidence.

Criminals and Police Treatment

Generally, the behaviour of the police towards offenders may depend more on the nature and types of personnel in police officialdom too. Thus, distinctions like young, old, mature and other factors may be determinant conditions in formulating the pattern of police behaviour towards offenders. Here, age or seniority of the police personnel is very important. They may have greater influence on the mode of behaviour of the police in actual contact and treatment of the offenders. On our enquiry as to whether there is any influence of the above mentioned criteria on maintaining a differential mode of behaviour among police towards offenders, a major part (73.6%) of the respondents had not seen any instance of consideration or concession in the actual behaviour of the police towards them as a result of the personality variation of police personnel. Only a minority (2.4%) of the sample felt that young officials were more considerate than others. A smaller group, i.e. 6.4 per cent of the respondents were of the opinion that old police officials are relatively more considerate towards them. However, 17.6 per cent of the respondents admitted that the local officials who already possess some kind of previous acquaintance with them and others on whom they had any other kind of influence due to political reasons or due to friendship, familial relationship, etc. were also considerate towards them in behaviour. As we have seen earlier, the age of the offender has a significant role in formulating these opinions. Here, also we analysed the data with respect to the age of the offenders as shown in Table 3.11.

Table 3.11

Difference in Treatment by the Police and Age of the Offenders

Difference in Police Treatment	*Age of the Offenders*				*Total*
	Below 30 years	*30-40 years*	*40-50 years*	*Above 50 years*	
No consideration/ critical	148 (73.6%)	47 (70,1%)	32 (80.0%)	16 (72.7%)	243 (73.6%)
Young officials are considerate	4 (2.0%)	3 (4.5%)	1 (2.5%)	—	8 (2.4%)
Old officials are considerate	11 (5.5%)	5 (7.5%)	3 (7.5%)	2 (9.1%)	21 (6.4%)
Other reasons (local official/previous acquaintance)	38 (18.9%)	12 (17.9%)	4 (10.0%)	4 (18.2%)	58 (17.6%)
Total	201 (100%)	67 (100%)	40 (100%)	22 (100%)	330 (100%)

It was seen that a majority (60.9%) of the offenders who felt that police were critical and had no consideration towards them in police dealings with them were aged under thirty years. Based on these findings it was further ascertained whether the respondents could experience any instance of differential behaviour by police personnel on the basis of distinctions like young or old, etc. in the study. It can be observed in the analysis that there was not much difference between the young and old officers in this aspect of possible differential behaviour as the response indicating the amount of consideration shown by those officials towards the offenders did not show much variation. However, a large majority (73.6%) of the sample of respondents felt that no such consideration was shown by the police. A majority (11 out of 21, i.e. 52.3%) of those who felt that old officials were considerate towards offenders were from among those who were under thirty years. This implies that old officials were at least considerate towards youngsters. This goes in close agreement with our earlier finding.

Further we enquired about the details on the attitude of the police towards the offenders with respect to the education of the respondents as education is also a determinant variable in this kind of relationship. Normally, educational status of the respondents can influence the behaviour of the police towards them in an indirect manner. In the assessment of certain situations also this counts a lot. On our examination of the data it was seen that though a section (43.9%) of the sample was having primary level of education, a majority (73.1%) of this group were felt that police behaviour was quite rough towards them. It was also

Table 3.12

Difference in Treatment by the Police and the Educational Background of Offenders

Difference in Police Treatment	*Educational Background of Offenders*				*Total*
	Illiterate	*Primary*	*Upper Primary*	*High School and Above*	
No consideration critical	58 (80.5%)	106 (73.1%)	50 (76.9%)	29 (60.4%)	243 (73.6%)
Young officials are considerate	2 (2.8%)	2 (1.4%)	2 (3.1%)	2 (4.2%)	8 (2.4%)
Old officials are considerate	1 (1.4%)	10 (6.9%)	4 (6.2%)	6 (12.5%)	21 (6.4%)
Considerate due to other reasons	11 (15.3%)	27 (18.6%)	9 (13.8%)	11 (22.9%)	58 (17.6%)
Total	72 (100%)	145 (100%)	65 (100%)	48 (100%)	330 (100%)

seen that the trend of feeling was more or less similar among the respondents from all educational levels as is clear from Table 3.12, even though there is a slight decline in percentages of respondents with such feelings as the level of education of respondents increases.

It was particularly seen that young officials in police force were more considerate towards those who had higher educational background. Young police officials were considerate only to 2.7 per cent of the illiterates whereas it increased to 4.2 per cent when educational level of the offenders increased to high school and above. The same phenomena was observed in the case of old officials also as is clear from Table 3.12. Among those who had experienced some kind of consideration from the police who were local official, who were familiar with them from previous acquaintance, their relationship, etc. also was found to increase with respect to the increase of educational level as judged from the percentage of responses.

While, 15.3 per cent of the illiterates experienced some kind of consideration from the police officials due to the above reasons, 22.9 per cent of the offenders having education of high school level and above experienced the same behaviour from the police officials. Following from the above it may be added that higher level of education of offender and the consequent modesty in the interaction with police is an important factor in establishing a relatively better police-offender relationship.

Very often the economic position of the respondents also may be an important point in studying the manifested behaviour of the police officials towards offenders. In our earlier analysis it was seen that the income background of the offenders also influences the attitude of the police towards the offenders. On our analysis of the present data with respect to the family income of the offenders and its influence on police treatment towards offenders, it was seen that a considerable majority (74.8%) of the middle income group (Rs 100 to 300 p.m.) had not experienced any kind of consideration from the police in their behaviour to the respondents. It was also interesting to note that young officials are relatively more considerate towards the offenders with a middle income background. A major portion (75.0%, i.e. 6 out of 8) of them who experienced some kind of consideration from young police officials belonged to the family income group of Rs 100 to 300 per month. As shown in Table 3.13 it can be seen that old officials are more considerate towards offenders from middle income group than young officials. This may suggest that economic background of the offenders and the response of the officials, especially the older generation of the officialdom, are very much related.

Table 3.13
Difference in Treatment by the Police and Family Income of the Offenders

Difference in Police Treatment	*Family Income (Rs)* 0-100 per Month	100-300 per Month	300-500 per Month	*Total*
No consideration/ critical	44 (74.6%)	184 (74.8%)	15 (60.0%)	243 (73.6%)
Young officials are considerate	2 (3.4%)	6 (2.4%)	—	8 (2.4%)
Old officials are considerate	2 (3.4%)	18 (7.3%)	1 (4.0%)	21 (6.4%)
Others are considerate due to other reasons	11 (18.6%)	38 (15.5%)	9 (36.0%)	58 (17.6%)
Total	59 (100%)	246 (100%)	25 (100%)	330 (100%)

It is possible that the attitude of the police can be under the influence of the history of punishment of the individuals too. Hence the data on the actual nature of police behaviour were analysed on these grounds to know how the police treatment varied with respect to the punishment. It was very clear from the analysis in Table 3.14 that longer involvement of respondents in subjecting to previous punishment was a special target of the police. It may be observed here that while 68.9 per cent of the first offenders could not experience any considerate behaviour from the police in their dealings, a still greater part of the sample (88.8%) of the offenders who had the longest history of punishment were in this category. In this connection we may recall our earlier findings that the police in Kerala are tempted to retain a prejudicial approach to the criminals, especially to the recidivists. Here an interesting aspect of our finding was that the police was quite capable of maintaining their inner sentiments and actual practice in conformity towards their dealings with the criminals. This was an important obser-

Table 3.14

Difference in Treatment from the Police and the History of Punishment of Offenders

Difference of Police Treatment	*History of Punishment*			*Total*
	No Previous Punishment	*Punished Once*	*Punished Twice and More*	
No consideration/ critical	158 (68.9%)	45 (80.5%)	40 (88.8%)	243 (73.6%)
Young officials are considerate	5 (2.2%)	1 (1.7%)	2 (4.5%)	8 (2.4%)
Old officials are considerate	17 (7.5%)	2 (3.4%)	2 (4.5%)	21 (6.4%)
Others are considerate due to other reasons	49 (21.4%)	8 (14.4%)	1 (2.2%)	58 (17.6%)
Total	229 (100%)	56 (100%)	45 (100%)	330 (100%)

vation. Table 3.14 shows that in this aspect of behaviour the young or the old officers in police service do not show much difference in attitude as is being explained by the findings of our analysis.

Police Brutality

So far we had discussed the police attitude towards offenders in general. The officials tatus of the policeman also may be a factor determining the mode of police behaviour towards offenders. The authority, power, status, etc. of the police official may vary according to the position in which he is functioning. Hence, we thought of studying the behaviour of the police with respect to the official position of police force. Their experience, skill and knowledge in dealing with different situations may have a definite role in moulding or shaping their strategy towards the offender. Hence we analysed the data on police behaviour as experienced by the offenders with respect to the hierarchy in the official status of officers. Here, it was seen that a majority (69.4%) of the sample experienced that officials belonging to subordinate level were more brutal in their behaviour towards the offenders. Among those who experienced brutal behaviour from the subordinates also a major part (54.6%) of offenders fell within the age group of twenty to thirty years. When the whole age group was viewed separately, 72.7% of the offenders admitted to experiencing brutal behaviour from subordinate police officials. Only a minority (16.7%) of the sample in this category admitted to experiencing considerate behaviour from the subordinates. An important aspect of this analysis is that police brutality varied with respect to the age of the offenders.

It was seen that the police brutality in behaviour to offenders by these sections of police was admitted by a relatively smaller percentage of older members. While 74.7 per cent of the offenders within the age of 30-40 years had suffered from police brutality in the sample, only 54.6 per cent of older respondents aged above fifty years were found to have the complaint. Similarly as it can be seen from Table 3.15, only 51.7 per cent of young offenders under twenty years had this kind of experience. Here again the police, especially the subordinate section, concentrated more on the youth in police brutality. This is an important aspect of our analysis.

In the context of these observations it is also quite relevant to examine whether the behaviour of the subordinate officials differed according to the income background of the offenders. The data was re-analysed on this principle and it was seen that a majority (69.4%) of the respondents had expressed that this section of the police officials were really brutal or very critical towards them in the first and all subsequent dealings. It was also observed from Table 3.16 that a good majority (70.7%) of the middle-income group of respondents in the sample had experienced brutal kind of behaviour from the subordinate

Table 3.15

Behaviour of the Subordinate Police Officials and the Age of the Offenders

Police Behaviour	*Age of Offenders*					*Total*
	Below 20 years	*20-30 years*	*30-40 years*	*40-50 years*	*Above 50 years*	
Brutal	15 (51.7%)	125 (72.7%)	50 (74.7%)	27 (67.5%)	12 (54.6%)	229 (69.4%)
Considerate	8 (27.6%)	24 (13.9%)	11 (16.4%)	7 (17.5%)	5 (22.7%)	55 (16.7%)
Others	6 (20.7%)	23 (13.4%)	6 (8.9%)	6 (15.0%)	5 (22.7%)	46 (13.9%)
Total	29 (100%)	172 (100%)	67 (100%)	40 (100%)	22 (100%)	330 (100%)

police officials. Details are given in Table 3.16. Here it is evident that regarding the behaviour of the subordinate police officials towards offenders, income does not have any influence on the police behaviour. Here while 66.1 per cent of lower-income respondents complained of police brutality, 64.0 per

Table 3.16
Behaviour of the Subordinate Police Officials and the Family Income of the Offenders

Police Behaviour	*Family Income (Rs)* 0-100 per Month	100-300 per Month	300-500 per Month	*Total*
Brutal	39 (66.1%)	174 (70.7%)	16 (64.0%)	229 (69.4%)
Considerate	15 (25.4%)	34 (13.8%)	6 (24.0%)	55 (16.7%)
Others	5 (8.5%)	38 (15.5%)	3 (12.0%)	46 (13.9%)
Total	59 (100%)	246 (100%)	25 (100%)	330 (100%)

Chi-square=6.82; DF=4
Table value at .05 level of significance=9.49.

cent of higher-income group also had a similar experience. The chi-square test also revealed that there is no significant relationship between income of respondents and the behaviour of the subordinate police. This shows that for the subordinates or lower level of police force income background of offenders is not a concern.

In the light of the foregoing discussion it is a matter of great interest to know whether the history of punishment at the background of the offenders can also influence the behaviour of the subordinate officials. It is quite possible that those victims who were exposed to previous history of punishment may have some kind of contact or acquaintance with the police officials, especially with subordinate officials in their career. In the present context this can be an efficient indicator of interactional behaviour between the units. It is interesting to note that among the first offenders themselves a good portion (64.2%) of them experienced brutality in behaviour from subordinate police officials.

It was also evident from the analysis that as the criminal background of the offender increased the nature of behaviour of the subordinate police officials towards them took a turn. Here it may be observed that while 86.7 per cent offenders who were convicted more than twice reported to have received brutality in behaviour from the above section of officials, only 64.2 per cent of the first offenders had this experience. It was further seen from the table that while 20.2 per cent of the first offenders experienced somewhat considerate behaviour from the subordinate officials, only 4.4 per cent of the respondents among those who were punished more than twice had this experience. The chi-square test also showed that there existed a significant relationship between police behaviour of the subordinate officials and the history of punishment of offenders at 5% level of confidence. Details are given in Table 3.17.

Table 3.17

Behaviour of the Subordinate Police Officials and History of Punishment of Offenders

Police Behaviour	*History of Punishment*			*Total*
	No Previous Punishment	*Punished Once*	*Punished Twice and More*	
Brutal	147 (64.2%)	43 (76.8%)	39 (86.7%)	229 (69.4%)
Considerate	48 (20.9%)	5 (8.9%)	2 (4.4%)	55 (16.7%)
Others	34 (14.9%)	8 (14.3%)	4 (8.9%)	46 (13.9%)
Total	229 (100%)	56 (100%)	45 (100%)	330 (100%)

Chi-square=12.79; DF=4
Table value at .05 level of significance=9.49

In many situations the behaviour of the police officials towards offenders may depend on their official status as well. In order to have a detailed understanding of the relationship, the data was re-analysed on these lines. First, we examined whether there was any influence of age of the offenders on the behaviour of the police officials. As shown in Table 3.18 it was seen that a major part (56.9%) of the offenders in the sample were of the opinion that the police officials were not much different from their colleagues in their behaviour towards the offenders.

Following from the analysis in Table 3.18, it may specifically be pointed here that while only 30 per cent of the respondents

Table 3.18

Behaviour of the Officials and Top Officials and Age of the Offenders

Police Behaviour	*Age of the Offenders*				*Total*
	Below 30 years	*30-40 years*	*40-50 years*	*Above 50 years*	
Brutal	118 (58.2%)	39 (58.2%)	24 (60.0%)	7 (31.8%)	188 (56.9%)
Considerate	41 (20.4%)	20 (29.9%)	12 (30.0%)	14 (63.6%)	87 (26.4%)
Others	42 (21.4%)	8 (11.9%)	4 (10.0%)	1 (4.6%)	55 (16.7%)
Total	201 (100%)	67 (100%)	40 (100%)	22 (100%)	330 (100%)

aged between 30-40 and 40-50 years in the sample experienced considerate behaviour towards them, as many as 63.6 per cent of the offenders who were older and aged above fifty years experienced this kind of behaviour. But on an assessment of police brutality it was invariably seen from the analysis that except in the case of older respondents the policy of behaviour appears to be more or less alike, as indicated by the percentages of respondents admitting so. Only 31.8 per cent of offenders aged above fifty years admitted to brutal behaviour from police, whereas majority of other smaller age groups felt the other way. Details are illustrated in Table 3.18.

On studying the relationship between official status of police officers and the income of the offenders in the police behaviour it was found that a major part (56.9%) of the respondents in the sample had experienced that the officers were brutal or rude in their behaviour to offenders. The analysis has not shown any kind of serious differences in this attitude of officers with respect to the differences in the income background of offenders (Table 3.19). As to the experiences of considerate behaviour also we can notice an increasing trend of percentage with an increase in income of respondents similar to the trend noted in the increase on the brutality of behaviour. Hence it is to be concluded here that the income of offenders is not an influential factor on the police

Table 3.19

Behaviour of the Officials and Top Officials and Family Income of Offenders

Police Behaviour	*Family Income (Rs)*			*Total*
	0-100 per Month	*100-300 per Month*	*300-500 per Month*	
Brutal	31 (52.6%)	142 (57.7%)	15 (60.0%)	188 (56.9%)
Considerate	14 (23.7%)	65 (26.4%)	8 (32.0%)	87 (26.4%)
Others	14 (23.7%)	39 (15.9%)	2 (8.0%)	55 (16.7%)
Total	59 (100%)	246 (100%)	25 (100%)	330 (100%)

brutality in behaviour among officers. In this regard our earlier finding on the behaviour of subordinates towards offenders as unrelated to the influence of income background of offenders is worth remembering.

On all those occasions, it is possible that the attitude of the officers towards offenders may have more influence in the behaviour with respect to their previous history or acquaintance in the context of criminal career. Hence, the data were analysed on these lines and it was found that among those respondents who had the history of punishment for more than twice, as large as 75.5 per cent of them admitted to suffering brutal behaviour from the officers during police custody, whereas only 52.4 per cent of the first offenders had this kind of experience during police confrontation, in the sample. As found from the present analysis only 26.0 per cent of the offenders could find the police officers considerate or liberal in their behaviour towards them.

Table 3.20

Behaviour of the Officials and Top Officials and the History of Punishment

Police Behaviour	*History of Punishment*			*Total*
	No Previous Punishment	*Punished Once*	*Punished Twice and More*	
Brutal	120 (52.4%)	34 (60.7%)	34 (75.5%)	188 (56.9%)
Considerate	69 (30.1%)	10 (17.9%)	8 (17.8%)	87 (26.4%)
Others	40 (17 5%)	12 (21.4%)	3 (6.7%)	55 (16.7%)
Total	229 (100%)	56 (100%)	45 (100%)	330 (100%)

In this group also a good majority (79.3%, i.e. 69 out of 87) of them were found to be first offenders whereas only 9.2 per cent (i.e. 8 out of 87) of those who had the career of punishment for more than twice could experience a considerate behaviour from police officers. As shown in Table 3.20 and following from our earlier findings it becomes very clear that the intensity of police brutality of officers in their behaviour increases with the increase in the history of punishment of the offender. It may further be noted that as indicated by the percentage of responses of offenders the officers also were found to be more liberal in their attitude and behaviour towards the first offenders. Here the real attitude and behaviour of the police towards criminals become all the more evident from our earlier and the present discussion.

Conclusion

In this chapter we have examined the various influential factors on the nature of police behaviour towards offenders.

Major variables examined here, include (1) education, (2) family income, (3) age, and (4) history of punishment. We have related the variables to the different dismensions of police behaviour including police brutality, biased behaviour of the police towards offenders physical torture, etc.

On the nature of police behaviour we found that educationally more backward respondents from the offenders found the police behaviour more (77.7%) intolerable than others. In terms of age of offenders it was brought out that the youth who were in the age group of twenty to thirty years were the extreme sufferers in experiencing the police behaviour as intolerable. In these relations the income background of the offenders was not found to be related much to the nature of police behaviour. There was not much difference in this aspect of the conclusion with respect to the different officials positions in police. In the study it was found that the police attitude towards the offender varied according to the previous history of punishment of the offender. With regard to the experience of physical torture by the offenders, the study brought out that relatively older offenders above fifty years were experiencing a comparatively light treatment than the youth within the age of 20-30 years. Young offenders under twenty years were also not serious sufferers in this. An important aspect of the present analysis is that the offender of longer previous history of punishment, i.e. twice and more were experiencing police brutality in a greater degree than others. Hence our hypothesis regarding the relationship between police behaviour on the one hand, and the socio-personal conditions of the offenders on the other stands verified.

4

THE POLICE AND PROFESSIONAL LIFE

Achievement of professionalism in service depends on the conditions of the professional and the profession. In the case of police service the significance of professionalism is relatively greater because its commitment to the service is twofold. The police system can attain its purpose only in the context of the wider society to which it caters. Police service acquires professional unity on the basis of the successful function of the police organization in society.

The criminal justice system bears the responsibility of controlling crime in society and of maintaining social order. To this challenge it reacts through various means and methods to prevent crime, either through deterrent actions or anticipatory behaviour. Deterrence, commonly involves reacting to alleged criminal incidents by investigating, arresting, prosecuting, convicting and punishing. Anticipatory activities involve detecting crime in advance of its commission. Such work is performed by the police, taking the form of preventive deployment as is being done by its beat patrol.

The basic functions of the police according to Alan R.Coffey are : (1) prevention of crime, (2) detection of crimes that have been committed, (3) identification of the person or persons responsible for crimes, (4) apprehension of person or persons responsible for crimes, (5) detection of the suspected offender or offenders for processing by the judiciary and (6) presentation of evidence to the prosecutor (Coffey, 1975 : 95). A conventional list of police duties would include: (1) protection of life and property, (2) preservation of the peace, (3) prevention of crime, (4) detection and arrest of violators of law, (5) enforcement of laws and ordinances, and (6) safeguarding the rights of the individuals (Bent and Rossam, 1976 : 3).

In this chapter the major discussion relates to the relationship between the attitudinal and professional factors of police personnel and success in the official career or the attainment of professionalism in service in the context of police-offender interactions.

The major hypothesis to be tested in this chapter is that the degree of contentment of the police in the profession is very much related to the nature of police career the officers maintain in service. These are generally indicated by the achievements of special credits by the officers in service by way of awards, prizes, rewards and special honours for distinguished service. These have been measured here in terms of education, length of service, age, motivation for joining police force, mode of response shown to reported offences, official status, etc. of the police officers. These have been empirically examined in the following pages.

Motivation

In any profession one's inclination or intention to opt for the same is very important especially regarding the targets of one's attainment of success in the career. Hence the selection of one's career depends on several factors. In the present study where the profession is more a sturdy one the members involved in it may have more definite consideration to go for them. In view of the special nature and functions of police service we thought of examining the motivation of our respondents to join the police service. Several studies have shown that the motivation behind joining the police force at large was the desire for superior status and special distinction among others in the society.

In the present study we have examined the nature of motivation of the respondents for joining the police department.

Accordingly when the data was analysed (Table 4.1) it was seen that a large portion (72.6%) of our police respondents were admitting that they came to the profession mainly as an employment. Only 27.4 per cent respondents said that they came to the police service due to the desire of enjoying better status in the society. Very often such ideas may vary with one's own intellectual and social background. In professional life, one's official status is important and hence, it was thought of examining the situation with respect to the official status of the respondents. It was found from the analysis that as large as 87.0 per cent of the subordinate police were attracted to the police service as a mere source of employment. On the other hand, it was quite interesting to note that majority (58.1%) of the officials and top officials in the sample were found to be motivated to find superior status in police service when they were coming first time to the profession.

Table 4.1

Official Status of the Respondents and the Motivation for Joining the Police

Motivation	*Official Status*		*Total*
	Subordinates	*Officials and Top Officials*	
As an employment	207 (87.0%)	47 (41.9%)	254 (72.6%)
Superior status in the society	31 (13.0%)	65 (58.1%)	96 (27.4%)
Total	238 (100%)	112 (100%)	350 (100%)

Chi-square value=77.6; DF=1
Table value at .05 level of significance=3.84
Pearson's coefficient of association=0 425.

Hence, it may be inferred from the analysis that while the subordinate officials in police looked upon the police as an ordinary career the officials and top officials in the police expected to have a dignified professional career through police service. The chi-square test also shows a significant relationship between the two variables. Pearson's coefficient of association showed good association between motivation and the official position of respondents in the study. Details are indicated in Table 4.1.

One's level of education and knowledge are important determinants in the formulation of attitudes towards the very life and particularly the future career or profession. Hence, the data were examined along these lines. Educational qualification of the respondents was found to influence their attitude towards the career. It was seen that a substantial part (86.7%) of those members who had the education of graduation and above had definite convictions about the profession. This group wanted to have dignified status positions in their official career. The attitude of the respondents of lower education was found to be quite different in the sample. As shown in Table 4.2, only 16.7 per cent of the respondents having education of SSLC and below were having motivation for better status through police

Table 4.2
Educational Level of the Respondents and Motivation for Joining the Police

Motivation	*Educational Level*			*Total*
	Below SSLC	*College Educated*	*Graduation and Above*	
As an employment	210 (83.3%)	38 (71.7%)	6 (13.3%)	254 (72.6%)
Superior status in the society	42 (16.7%)	15 (28.3%)	39 (86.7%)	96 (27.4%)
Total	252 (100%)	53 (100%)	45 (100%)	350 (100%)

Chi-square value=94.4; DF=2
Table value at .05 level of significance=5.99
Pearson's coefficient association=0.460.

career, whereas the remaining 83.3 per cent of this group resorted to this profession just for an employment. It can also be seen that a still greater (28.3%) percentage of college-educated respondents look upon police career as a source of status. Hence, it is very clear that the role of education is more important in creating a professionally status-conscious group in police service. Details are given in Table 4.2. The chi-square test shows significant relationship between motivation and educational background of the respondents. Pearson's coefficient of association also shows good association between the two variables.

Police Response to Cases

Sincerity and devotion to the service is very important to judge about one's commitment and involvement in the profession. These are quite basic to the conditions of attainment of professional development. In order to study the different channels of development of professionalism among the police in their work it was thought of examining the approach of the police towards various situations where violation of law or offenses occur in the society. The response shown by the police towards reports of incidences relating to offences may be an indicator of the degree of professional interest and capacity of the officials. Hence, it was decided to analyse the details and accordingly the data available on the quickness of response of the police towards reported offences were examined and it was found that majority (64.3%) of the police in the study attended to reported cases immediately. Only in the remaining 35.7 per cent cases, the police had to wait for orders from superior sources to initiate action. Under modern conditions, where the bureaucracy assumes new dimensions of policy implementation in the context of various emerging factors like political,

Table 4.3

Official Status of the Respondents and the Mode of Response on Reported Cases

Mode of Response	*Official Status*		*Total*
	Subordinate Officials	*Officials and Top Officials*	
Immediate action	115 (48.3%)	110 (98.2%)	225 (64.3%)
Wait to get orders from the superiors	123 (51.7%)	2 (1.8%)	125 (35.7%)
Total	238 (100%)	112 (100%)	350 (100%)

Table 4.4

Age of the Police Officiers and the Mode of Response on Reported Cases

Mode of Response	*Age of Officials*				*Total*
	20-30 years	*30-40 years*	*40-50 years*	*Above 50 years*	
Immediate action	11 (23.4%)	80 (55.9%)	85 (81.0%)	49 (89.1%)	225 (64.3%)
Wait to get orders from the superiors	36 (76.6%)	63 (41.1%)	20 (19.0%)	6 (10.9%)	125 (35.7%)
Total	47 (100%)	143 (100%)	105 (100%)	55 (100%)	350 (100%)

Chi-square value=66.63; DF=3

Table value at .05 level of significance=7.82

Pearson's coefficient of association=.399

administrative, etc., it is quite natural that the executive or the ministerial services tend to be more flexible in carrying out functions. Thus, in police service also the quickness of responding to reported cases or complaints on issues being a matter of urgency from the point of social need, it was thought of examining the data with respect to the official position of the police. As detailed in Table 4.3 among the officials and top officials as many as 98.2 per cent of the respondents admitted to initiating action immediately on getting the report to the police whereas only 48.3 per cent of the subordinate officials responded to the cases immediately. Here it may be seen that among the subordinate officials, a majority (51.7%) of them waited for orders from superior sources to initiate action on reported cases. This may perhaps be a question of administrative issue, but in the very same analysis 48.3 per cent of the subordinate officials immediately responded to the cases. Here, the special role of the senior officials, namely, officials and top officials in taking active immediate interest of the police towards the needs of the society has been found to be quite remarkable.

As the nature and amount of experience in life and service may be a factor influencing one's ability to respond to such services age also can be one of the determinants of such functions. Hence in our further analysis, the nature of response shown by the police towards reported cases on offences on the basis of the age of the police officials, it was found that a good majority (64.3%) of them said that they had taken immediate action to the reported cases of offences in their respective jurisdictions. It may be observed from Table 4.4 that while 89.1 per cent of officers in the highest age group, namely those aged fifty years and above could take immediate action on reported cases, only 23.4 per cent of the officials in the lowest (20-30 years) age group could resort to immediate action. It can also be seen that while as many as 76.6 per cent of the officers in their twenties waited for orders from superiors for initiating action, only 10.9 per cent of the officials in the highest age group waited for such instructions. From this it is very clear that older officers were more bold and responsive to the protective needs of the society. This of course may be due to the experience and authority that they might have wielded from relatively longer service and experience they had derived from their police career. The chi-square test showed significant relationship between the mode of response and age of the police officials in this regard. Pearson's coefficient also showed relatively better association between the variables.

On all these occasions, service or life experiences alone will not be able to explain the situations of decision-making. One's ability in such critical conditions may well depend on the educational background also as education enables an individual more for a lucrative job and decision-making. Hence, the data were analysed on the basis of the educational conditions of the respondents. As shown in Table 4.5 it was found that officers with higher education could react to the situations more quickly than others. 95.3 per cent of the officers with the educational qualification of graduation and above indicated that they had taken decisions immediately on reported cases of offenses. Among those who waited for the orders from above for initiating enquiry, judging from the respective educational backgrounds very few (4.7%) of the highly educated members were found to have postponed the decisions to a later occasion to get orders from above. Thus, the role of higher education and prompt immediate attention of the police on reported cases in their respective jurisdiction are very much related.

Table 4.5
Educational Level of the Officers and the Mode of Response on Reported Cases

Mode of Response	*Educational Level*			*Total*
	Below SSLC	*College Educated*	*Graduation and above*	
Immediate action	155 (61.5%)	28 (52.8%)	42 (95 3%)	225 (64.3%)
Wait to get orders from the superiors	97 (38.5%)	25 (47.2%)	3 (4.7%)	125 (35.7%)
Total	252 (100%)	53 (100%)	45 (100%)	350 (100%)

Following from the preceding observation and approaching the problem in a more precise manner it may be pointed out here that one's length of service of career in officialdom or amount of experience is a potent phenomenon in the problem of professionalism of police. On occasions where self-initiative, leadership and authority become necessary as in the case of

Table 4,6

Length of Service of the Officers and the Mode of Response on Reported Cases

Mode of Response	*Length of Services* Below 10 years	10 to 20 years	Above 20 years	*Total*
Immediate action	29 (33.0%)	80 (60.6%)	116 (89.2%)	225 (64 3%)
Wait to get orders from the superiors	59 (67.0%)	52 (39.4%)	14 (10.8%)	125 (35.7%)
Total	88 (100%)	132 (100%)	130 (100%)	350 (100%)

Chi-square value=73.70; DF=2
Table value at .05 level of significance=5.99
Pearson's coefficient of association=0.417

police, the role of official career emerges as a very significant factor.

Accordingly, on analysis of the data, it was seen from Table 4.6 that a sufficiently large amount (89.2%) of respondents who had put in more than twenty years of service could initiate action and dispose of the cases immediately, whereas only 33.0 per cent of the officials who had put in less than ten years of service in the police career could respond to the cases without any delay. While only a few (10.8%) of more experienced members waited for orders from above to initiate action, a majority (67.0%) of the respondents having a service of less than ten years had postponed their action for want of orders from above. This observation is a pointer to the fact that longer experience in service of the officials adds to the sincerity and efficiency of the police especially in dealing with reported cases of offences. The chi-square test also showed significant relationship between length of service of respondents and mode of response to reported cases.

As a step further in the study of professionalism of the police officials the extent of involvement of the officers in dealing with the crime and criminal needs to be examined. Here, during this process the police may very often face problems on meeting situations involving offenders. In order to explain some aspects of the problem it was thought of studying whether there was any difficulty experienced by the officers in dealing with the offenders. Accordingly when the data were analysed with respect to the official status of the respondents as detailed in Table 4.7, it was found that a good majority (75.7%) of the police experienced no difficulties in their initial dealings with offenders. Here an important observation forthcoming from the analysis is that with regard to the absence of difficulties in initial dealings with offenders by the police, there was not much difference in the experiences among members belonging to different official categories. The result of the chi-square test showed that the official status of the police and the experience of difficulties in the initial tackling of offenders are unrelated.

Table 4.7
Officials Status of the Officers and the Difficulties in Tackling the Offenders

Experience of Difficulties	*Official Status*		*Total*
	Subordinates	*Officials and Top Officials*	
No difficulties experienced	184 (77.3%)	81 (72.3%)	265 (75.7%)
Difficulties experienced	54 (22.7%)	31 (27.7%)	85 (24.3%)
Total	238 (100%)	112 (100%)	350 (100%)

Chi-square value=1.03; DF=1
Table value at .05 level of significance=3.84.

It was doubtful whether problems or difficulties in tackling offenders may be influenced by one's experience in service or career. Accordingly in order to have an answer to this question the observations on the problems or difficulties if any confronted by the police were analysed with respect to the length of service of the police in the profession, and it was observed that 81.8 per cent of those officials who had less than ten years of standing in the profession could find no difficulties in tackling the offenders. On the other hand, in the case of officers having a still greater service, i.e. above twenty years, 68.5 per cent of them did not experience any difficulty. It could

Table 4.8
Length of Service of the Respondents and Difficulties they Experienced in Tackling Offenders

Difficulties Experienced	*Length of Service* *Below 10 years*	*10-20 years*	*Above 20 years*	*Total*
No difficulties experienced	72 (81.8%)	104 (78.8%)	89 (68.5%)	265 (75.7%)
Difficulties experienced	16 (18.2%)	28 (21.2%)	41 (31.5%)	85 (24.3%)
Total	88 (100%)	132 (100%)	130 (100%)	350 (100%)

Chi-square value=6.18; DF=2
Table value at .05 level of significance=5.99.

be found from the analysis in Table 4.8 that greater the amount of service that officers had greater were the difficulties experienced in tackling the situation. This implies that the beginners in the police force took up the venture in a more honest and challenging manner than the officials of more service who may quite often take the situations as simple when they are not.

Moreover a longer experience or service in the same trade alone need not be a criterion for effective performance in career. One's skill, knowledge, and effective training are other pertinent factors associated with this. In this situation beginners in service who are fresh from their educational and training background may well be able to compete with others more efficiently.

In the context of the foregoing observations it would be all the more relevant to examine the relationship of the age of the officers with their efficiency in tackling situations. Here the role of youngsters in contrast to that of older members in the official cadre can normally reflect the real efficiency and ability of the service. Accordingly, from the analysis it followed that fewer older respondents experienced no difficulties in the police-criminal confrontation than the youngsters. While 61.8 per cent of the officers who were above fifty years of age had no difficulty in the sample, there were as many as 80.9 per cent of young officers who belonged to the age group of twenty to thirty years who ruled out any instance of difficulty in their experience with offenders. This kind of attitude reflected among the older members or members having more service in the profession compared to the youngsters or beginners is a unique feature observed in the present sample of study. This reflects well on the professional life of the police in our enquiry. Details of the analysis are given in Table 4.9.

Table 4.9

Age of the Officers and Experience of Difficulties in Tackling Offenders

	Age of the Officials				
Difficulties Experienced	*20-30 years*	*30-40 years*	*40-50 years*	*Above 50 years*	*Total*
No difficulties experienced	38 (80.9%)	113 (79.0%)	80 (76.2%)	34 (61.8%)	265 (75.7%)
Difficulties experienced	9 (19.1%)	30 (21.0%)	25 (23.8%)	21 (38.2%)	85 (24.3%)
Total	47 (100%)	143 (100%)	105 (100%)	55 (100%)	350 (100%)

Disposal of Cases

The professional equipment and the success of the executive is an important indicator of the efficiency of the strategies for overcoming obstacles in carrying out one's duties, especially those requiring skill. This is more important in an executive cader like the police. It has been often doubted as to how and why the disposal of cases of offences are delayed in the society.

Hence, it was thought of examining the situation in the context of police service. Thus, we analysed the major reasons for the pending cases as expressed by the police officials. It was found that 47.1 per cent of the respondents were of the opinion that there was no case pending for investigation under them. Among the major reasons for the delay in disposal of cases, as revealed by them, important ones were the lack of co-operation from society, and the intervention and pressures on police officers at different levels, and influences from still higher sources of the state machinery.

In our investigation 45.4 per cent of the police officials were of the opinion that the non-co-operative attitude of the public towards the police in investigating the cases was the main reason for pending investigations. Only a minority (7.4%) of the police officials in the sample were of the opinion that the delay in investigations of offences was due to the intervention and pressures of police officials and from higher sources. It was also evident that those who were not getting co-operation from the public, a major portion (73.0%) of them were subordinates. This may be due to the fact that the public were not co-operating with the subordinate police officials. This is an important point in the police career and police-community relationship.

Table 4.10
Official Status of the Officers and the Reason for Pending Police Investigation on Offences

Reasons	*Official Status*		*Total*
	Subordinates	*Officials and Top Officials*	
No instance	106 (44.5%)	59 (52.7%)	165 (47.2%)
Lack of co-operation from society	116 (48.7%)	43 (38.4%)	159 (45.4%)
Intervention and pressures from police officials and higher sources	16 (6.7%)	10 (8.9%)	26 (7.4%)
Total	238 (100%)	112 (100%)	350 (100%)

It may also be noted that subordinate officials were having primary contact with the public. Hence, the non-co-operation from them may also be due to the peculiar kind of behaviour of the subordinate police officials towards the public. Many a time an arrogant authoritative approach may not be relished by the masses. The details are given in Table 4.10.

It may specially be observed in the analysis that those officials who had experienced a delay in disposing of cases due to the intervention and pressures from higher sources, a majority (16 out of 26, i.e. 61.5%) were subordinates. However, 8.9 per cent of the officials and top officials also admitted that there was delay in disposal of cases due to these reasons.

We further examined the data with respect to the length of service of the officials in the study. As revealed in Table 4.11, a majority (53.1%) of the officials who had more than twenty years of service in the police, were of the opinion that there was no case pending disposal in their jurisdiction. On the other hand, those who had below ten years of service in the police department, a majority (54.5%) of the respondents were of the opinion that the delay in police investigation was due to the non-co-operative attitude of the public towards the police.

Table 4.11

Length of Service of the Respondents and Reasons for Pending Police Investigation on Offences

Reasons	*Length of Service*			*Total*
	Below 10 years	*10-20 years*	*Above 20 years*	
No instance	32 (36.4%)	64 (48.5%)	69 (53.1%)	165 (47.2%)
Lack of co-operation from society	48 (54.5%)	56 (42.4%)	55 (42.3%)	159 (45.4%)
Intervention and pressures from police officials and higher sources	8 (9.1%)	12 (9.1%)	6 (4.6%)	26 (7.4%)
Total	88 (100%)	132 (100%)	130 (100%)	350 (100%)

This part of the analysis showed that among the officers who felt that the delay in disposing cases of offences was basically due to the intervention and pressures from higher officials, a large (18 out of 26, i.e. 69.2%) section of respondents were from among those who had put in more than ten years of standing in the profession. It may be pointed out here that the beginners are looking up the society or community around to give more efficient service to the public than other sections of police machinery.

Escape from Police Charge

It has been often found that the offender escapes from punishment in certain situations. Even in the matter of reported cases though there were so many difficulties in investigation as lack of adequate staff, vehicle facilities and modern amenities for making quick on-the-spot enquiries, the percentage of conviction was found to be very low. Usually, such conditions need not be due to the fact of non-commitment of these offences but because of the fact that the prosecution could not succeed in giving adequate evidence that the accused is guilty of the offence. We sought the opinion of police officials also in this matter. Accordingly, we found that a majority (55.4%) of the officers were of the opinion that the offenders were escaping from punishment due mainly to the fact of influencing the witness by the parties concerned or the non-co-operation of the witnesses in relevant situations. These influences very often reported to be exercised through bribes or through other sources of manipulation. It is widely reported that political influence on police officials through politicians on these cases was a main reason for the escape of the real offenders from police charge and thereby from the channels of punishment. Our finding that 18.6 per cent of the police officials in the sample were pointing out that the offenders were escaping from police charge shows clearly that political and other kind of pressures are in operation.

On our examination of the same phenomenon with respect to the official status of ther espondents, it was seen that among those who were of the opinion that the offenders were escaping from punishment by giving bribe to the police officials a good majority of them (21 out of 26, i.e. 80.8%) were subordinate officials. But 50.0 per cent of the subordinate officials in the sample were of the opinion that lack of adequate witnesses, influences exerted on the available witnesses, and indifference on the part of the witnesses were the main reasons for paving the way for the escape of offenders from punishment. Among officials and top officials in the sample also a majority (66.9%) of them agreed with this view. Details of the analysis are revealed in Table 4.12.

Table 4.12

Official Status of the Police Officers and their Opinion about the Ground of Escape of Offenders from Police Charge

Ground of Escape	*Official Status*		
	Subordinates	*Officials and Top Officials*	*Total*
Bribe to officials	21 (8.8%)	5 (4.5%)	26 (7.4%)
Bribe to witnesses	119 (50.0%)	75 (66.9%)	194 (55.4%)
External and political pressure	66 (27.7%)	25 (22.3%)	91 (26.0%)
Others	32 (13.4%)	7 (6.3%)	39 (11.2%)
Total	238 (100%)	112 (100%)	350 (100%)

On enquiring the channels of influence reaching the witnesses, a majority of the police officials (55.4%) were of the opinion that the escape of offenders occurs as a result of bribing the witnesses. In our study 62.5 per cent respondents from among the beginners having less than ten years of service in the profession had the above view.

Officers having a longer career also maintained more or less similar attitudes as the percentages did not show much variation as is evident from Table 4.13.

Table 4.13

Length of Service of the Police Officers and their Opinion on the Ground of Escape of Offenders from Police Charge

Ground of Escape	*Length of Service*			*Total*
	Below 10 years	*10-20 years*	*Above 20 years*	
Bribe to officials	6 (6.8%)	8 (6.1%)	12 (9.2%)	26 (7.4%)
Bribe to witnesses	55 (62.5%)	60 (45.4%)	79 (60.8%)	194 (55.4%)
External and political pressures	14 (15.9%)	43 (32.6%)	34 (26.2%)	91 (26.0%)
Others	13 (14.8%)	21 (15.9%)	5 (3.8%)	39 (11.2%)
Total	88 (100%)	132 (100%)	130 (100%)	350 (100%)

In any society the control of crime and offences and the establishment of a social order is the main intention of the police force. A control of the law and order situation is the real indicator of the efficiency of the police. Political unrest, processions, demonstrations, unemployment, student unrest, youth violence, increasing labour problems, and other very common issues create a lot of difficulties for the police in maintaining law and order situation in the society. They are very much related to the day-to-day functioning of both the police and the society. Hence, a real assessment of police professionalism needs to be carried out with respect to the extent to which the police have succeeded in maintaining law and order. This may illustrate further how the police have developed and succeeded in maintaining their professional interests and responsibilities. As a measure of this the difference, if any, experienced by the police in tackling the situation was studied to assess the nature of confrontation of the police to the situation of offences which would certainly be a good indicator of the professional interest and ability that the police maintain. Hence, these facts were studied from the data.

It was observed that a majority (54.6%) of the respondents expressed that they faced several difficulties in controlling offences and in bringing back a normal situation and occasions of revolts in their jurisdiction. For many this was not an easy task. On our analysis of the data with respect to the official status of the police cadre among the respondents it was found that a major part (53.6%) of officials and top officials had found no difficulty in tackling situations of that kind, whereas 58.4 per cent of the subordinates had experienced one or other kind of difficulties as revealed by the present analysis (Table 4.14).

Table 4.14

Official Status of the Police and Difficulties in Maintaining Law and Order Situation under their Jurisdiction

Experience of Difficulties	*Official Status*		*Total*
	Subordinates	*Official and Top Officials*	
Difficulties Experienced	139 (58.4%)	52 (46.4%)	191 (54.6%)
No difficulties experienced	99 (41.6%)	60 (53.6%)	159 (45.4%)
Total	238 (100%)	112 (100%)	350 (100%)

Hence, the confidence and ability of the higher cadres in maintaining the law and order situation is certainly a good achievement from the point of view of professional equipment of the police force. In the case of subordinates also a section (41.6%) of the respondents had not experienced any difficulty, as understood from our study.

Many a time professional attainments are the functions of one's educational achievement as education helps to equip the individual more on a sound basis through special training and knowledge in the field. Hence, we examined our data with respect to the educational background of the respondents as shown in Table 4.15. It was found from the sample that among those having below SSLC qualification, a major part (58.3%)

admitted to experiencing difficulties in maintaining law and order under their jurisdiction whereas among the more educated group, i.e. those with college education and above, 50.9 per cent had not experienced any kind of difficulty in handling the

Table 4.15

Educational Level of the Police and their Experience of Difficulties in Maintaining Law and Order in their Jurisdiction

Experience of Difficulties	*Educational Level*			*Total*
	Below SSLC	*College Educated*	*Graduation and Above*	
Difficulties experienced	147 (58.3%)	26 (49.1%)	18 (40 0%)	191 (54.6%)
No difficulties experienced	105 (41.7%)	27 (50.9%)	27 (60.0%)	159 (45.4%)
Total	252 (100%)	53 (100%)	45 (100%)	350 (100%)

law and order situation as they have expressed in the study. It is also interesting to note that among those who had an educational attainment of graduation and above, a good majority (60%) were not understood to have experienced any such problem in maintaining law and order in their area.

Hence it is clear from the analysis that the educational background of the officials does influence the performance of the duties of police especially in dealing with issues of law and order problems in society. In this context, it may be recalled that the previous finding where the officials and top officials faced little difficulty in tackling cases. It is quite common that more educated members are likely to be in superior cadres, particularly when more members are recruited directly through all-India services and other competitive examinations wherein higher education plays a very vital role. Hence, it may be added here that those who are more educated perform the task more efficiently than those who are less educated. The chi-square test also showed that there was a significant relationship between the level of education of the respondents and experience of difficulties in establishing law and order in their jurisdiction.

On several occasions difficulties experienced by the police may vary according to the age of the officer concerned. Those who are young and have had little experience in the field of policy implementation may possibly experience more difficulties than a more aged and experienced person in service matters. Hence we examined the data on the basis of the age of police officials. It was found that while 59.6 per cent of those who were in the age group of below thirty years experienced difficulties in maintaining law and order, a majority (52.7%) of those who were above fifty years of age had no such problems in controlling revolts and similar situations in society, and to establish law and order. Further as can be seen from the analysis in Table 4.16 it is clear that more aged members found that it was more easy for them to handle tough situations than youngsters.

Table 4.16

Age of the Police and Experience of Difficulties in Maintaining Law and Order in their Jurisdiction

Experience of Difficulties	*Age of the Police Officials* 20-30 years	30-40 years	40-50 years	Above 50 years	*Total*
Difficulties experienced	28 (59.6%)	76 (53.1%)	61 (58.1%)	26 (47.3%)	191 (54.6%)
No difficulties experienced	19 (40.4%)	67 (46.9%)	44 (41.9%)	29 (52.7%)	159 (45.4%)
Total	47 (100%)	143 (100%)	105 (100%)	55 (100%)	350 (100%)

As we have already seen, the extent of one's service in the police department will certainly be an influential factor on one's performance of official duties. Hence we took up the issue for analysing the approach of the officials towards facing problems of law and order, and accordingly, it was seen that among those who had less than ten years of official career, a major portion (67.1%) were found to experience difficulties in maintaining law and order. The same is true with respect to those who had ten to twenty years of service to their credit. Among these members, 59.1 per cent of respondents had met with difficulties in handling disturbances in law and order situations. However, this phenomenon varied considerably in the case of those who had more than twenty years of service. A majority (58.5%) of these officials had not experienced any difficulty in dealing with offences in their jurisdiction as found from the study.

It was seen that as a whole greater service in the profession was an instrumental factor in enabling the officials to tackle the situations to satisfy the needs of the society than the relatively less experienced members in the sample. As the service in the department increases the difficulty experienced by the officials in maintaining law and order was found to be on a decreasing trend. Details are given in Table 4.17.

Table 4.17

Length of Service of the Police and their Experience of Difficulties in Maintaining Law and Order in their Jurisdiction

Experience of Difficulties	*Length of Service*			*Total*
	Below 10 years	*10-20 years*	*Above 20 years*	
Difficulties experienced	59 (67.1%)	78 (59.1%)	54 (41.5%)	191 (54.6%)
No Difficulties experienced	29 (32.9%)	54 (40.9%)	76 (58.5%)	159 (45.4%)
Total	88 (100%)	132 (100%)	130 (100%)	350 (100%)

Though a section of the respondents, as we have already observed, were motivated to join the police for mere employment, on our enquiry of their opinion about the profession, it was brought out that a major part (65.7%) of the sample had the opinion that their profession was a pleasant and rewarding one. It was also noted that among the officials and top officials in the sample as many as 84.8 per cent of the respondents had the same attitude. Hence, in the light of this observation it may be asserted that the higher officials in police service looked upon their profession as a pleasant and rewarding one than the subordinates. Details are expressed in Table 4.18.

Table 4.18

Official Status of the Respondents and their Opinion about their Profession

Opinions about the Profession	*Official Status*		*Total*
	Subordinates	*Officials and Top Officials*	
Pleasant and rewarding	135 (56.7%)	95 (84.8%)	230 (65.7%)
Not pleasant and rewarding	103 (43.3%)	17 (15.2%)	120 (34.3%)
Total	238 (100%)	112 (100%)	350 (100%)

On enquiry about new experiences of the police in their profession it is quite natural that the age of the respondents may have a significant influence in their assessment about the past experiences, and the trends of present official career. Accordingly, on examination of the present sample on the basis of the age of our respondents we found that a major part of the youngsters (57.4%) who were in the age group of twenty to thirty years were of the opinion that their profession was quite pleasant and rewarding whereas a still larger (80.0%) section of the older members who had crossed the age of fifty years had the same view. A minor section (34.3%) of the sample could not agree with the above view. This attitude was found to be decreasing as the age of the respondents increased. In other words, it is to be inferred from the analysis that the more aged respondents derived relatively greater amount of contentment in their career than younger members. This difference in attitude may possibly be due to the difference in the degree of integration of youngsters into the police system. Details are given in Table 4.19

As everywhere else, the police service also does not seem to be free from its usual official problems: problems of corrup-

Table 4.19
Age of the Respondents and Opinion about their Profession

Opinion on the Profession	*Age of Respondents*				*Total*
	20-30 years	*30-40 years*	*40-50 years*	*Above 50 years*	
Pleasant and rewarding	27 (57.4%)	84 (58.7%)	75 (71.4%)	44 (80,0%)	230 (65.7%)
Not pleasant and rewarding	20 (42.6%)	59 (41.3%)	30 (28.6%)	11 (20.0%)	120 (34.3%)
Total	47 (100%)	143 (100%)	105 (100%)	55 (100%)	350 (100%)

tion, brutality, misconduct, etc. in modern times. Even under these conditions one's meritorious and distinguished contribution to the service and nation by the police have been well-recognized and honoured by giving special rewards and distinctions. It was a matter of interest to examine the details of acquiring distinction by the police as a test of the recognition of the professional equipment of the police. This aspect of the problem was studied from the present sample and it was found that 61.4 per cent (i.e. 215 out of 350) of our respondents had achieved one or other kind of distinction like good service entry or other rewards. However, 44.3 per cent of them were understood to have been honoured by special rewards. 17.1 per cent of the respondents have received good service entry for their meritorious service. Distinctions in service and recognition of their merit very often constitute a special credit in the span of one's officialdom. This is more significant in executive cadres like police, military, etc. This certainly is an indicator of the spirit of professionalism.

Hence it will be appropriate to study the conditions of these special credits to explain the details on professional life of police. Thus when the data were studied from Table 4.20, it was seen that a majority (52.7%) of the senior officials in the sample have a history of obtaining one or other kind of awards. In the case of subordinate employees in the sample only 40.3 per cent of the respondents could secure those distinctions.

On a more detailed enquiry it was brought out that while 30.4 per cent of the senior officials secured good service

Table 4.20
Official Status of the Respondents and Achievements of Credits

Credits Achieved	*Official Status*		*Total*
	Subordinates	*Officials and Top Officials*	
None	116 (48.8%)	19 (16.9%)	135 (38.6%)
Good service entry	26 (10.9%)	34 (30.4%)	60 (17.1%)
Rewards/Awards	96 (40.3%)	59 (52.7%)	155 (44.3%)
Total	238 (100%)	112 (100%)	350 (100%)

entry for their distinguished service only a few (10.9%) of subordinates were found to be successful in winning similar distinctions. Thus it was clear that it was the senior officials who took the lead in winning more distinctions by virtue of their contribution to police service. These indeed add to their ability and equipment in service.

Gainful experience and the professional satisfaction of employees is an important concern in a job-oriented life. Here chances of getting personal experiences or one's age can influence

Table 4.21
Age of the Respondents and Achievements of Credits

Credits Achieved	*Age of Respondents*				*Total*
	20-30 years	*30-40 years*	*40-50 years*	*Above 50 years*	
None	33 (70.2%)	75 (52.4%)	25 (23.8%)	2 (3.6%)	135 (38.6%)
Good service entry	6 (12.7%)	16 (11.2%)	23 (21.9%)	15 (27.3%)	60 (17.1%)
Awards/Rewards	8 (17.1%)	52 (36.4%)	57 (54.3%)	38 (69.1%)	155 (44.3%)
Total	47 (100%)	143 (100%)	105 (100%)	55 (100%)	350 (100%)

official life to a great extent in one's career. One's competitive performance enables the individual to attain special credits. Consideration on knowledge and continued experience in the special field, etc. wield more popularity in society and in one's official career. Hence in order to study the influence of age on one's professional attainment, it was thought of examining the present data with respect to the age structure of our respondents. Analysis from Table 4.21 revealed that a major part (69.1%) of the respondents above the age of fifty years had won special awards during their official career. Whereas among the youngsters who were between the age of twenty to thirty years only 17.0 per cent of the respondents could secure similar credits. Though 27.3 per cent of the members aged above fifty years in the sample could obtain good service entry during their official career, only 12.7 per cent of respondents from the youngest age group in the sample had recorded the receipt of this distinction. It may be seen from the analysis that age plays an important role in the attainment of special credits in service. This may perhaps be mainly due to the larger amount of opportunities open to the older members in comparison to those of younger officers. Hence it needs to be pointed out here that younger members particularly those who are between the ages of twenty to thirty years are to be specially credited professionally as they have established themselves for official recognition of their merit at a relatively younger age.

The service background of the police officials in the department also, to a great extent, influences the achievement of credits in service. Hence an attempt was made to find out the details on the basis of the length of service of the respondents in the sample. By way of the results of this analysis it may be stated that among those who were having less than ten years of service to their credit 70.4 per cent respondents had not received any distinction during the tenure of their service whereas among those who had more than twenty years of service in the profession 64.6 per cent of them had succeeded in securing distinctions and rewards for their valuable service in the profession. It is quite interesting to note that the frequency of acquiring distinctions or rewards was found to increase with the increase in the service of respondents in the police profession.

Hence it is to be inferred that those who had more service in the police profession, work more efficiently and execute their duties in a more rewarding manner than the beginners. In this connection it is quite pertinent to recall the findings on the beginners in service in police. It is to be added here that it might be a marvellous beginning which makes for experience and enables

Table 4.22

Length of Service of the Respondents and Achievements of Credits during the Tenure of their Service in Police Department

Credits Achieved	*Length of Service*			*Total*
	Below 10 years	*10-20 years*	*Above 20 years*	
None	62 (70.4%)	52 (39.4%)	21 (16.2%)	135 (38.6%)
Good service entry	13 (14.8%)	22 (16.7%)	25 (19.2%)	60 (17.1%)
Rewards	13 (14.8%)	58 (43.9%)	84 (64.6%)	155 (44.3%)
Total	88 (100%)	132 (100%)	130 (100%)	350 (100%)

Chi-square value=70.28; DF=4
Table value at .05 level of significance=9.49
Pearson's coefficient of association=0.409

up the beginner to procure high distinctions and rewards which will also be a credit to the society. The chi-square test also showed a significant relationship between length of service and procuring distinction as a recognition of their service. Pearson's coefficient showed good association between the variables. Details are given in Table 4.22.

Career Satisfaction

Though there are evternal interferences and influences of many kinds from several sources on the police in their official duties especially where they have to face many other problems during their regular work it is a matter of serious concern whether the police get any chance of contentment in their career.

This is more important when the nature and condition of risk involved in their work are also taken into consideration. The contentment in the work and job satisfaction are certainly related to professional interest and stability. Hence we thought of enquiring of our respondents about their opinion on their career and contentment. We found that a good majority (62.6%)

Table 4.23
Official Status of the Police and their Contentment with the Career

Feeling of Contentment	*Official Status*		*Total*
	Subordinates	*Officials and Top Officials*	
Contented with police career	125 (52.5%)	94 (83.9%)	219 (62.6%)
Discontented due to heavy work	40 (16.8%)	6 (5.4%)	46 (13.1%)
Discontented due to bad service conditions	52 (21.8%)	5 (4.5%)	57 (16.3%)
Discontented due to bad behaviour of superiors	21 (8.8%)	7 (6.2%)	28 (8.0%)
Total	238 (100%)	112 (100%)	350 (100%)

Chi-square value=34.34; DF=3
Table value at .05 level of significance=7.82
Table value at .01 level of significance=11.34

of them were of the opinion that they were contented with the police career. Only 16.3 per cent of the respondents expressed that they were not contented with their career. This was mainly due to the bad service conditions. 13.1 per cent of the respondents were not pleased with the profession due to the heavy work they had to do in the department. A few (8.0%) of the respondents in the sample expressed that due to bad behaviour of the superiors they were thoroughly dissatisfied with the present work.

From a detailed analysis of our data with respect to the official position of the respondents it was found that while only slightly more than half (52.5%) of the subordinates were satisfied with the police career, a good majority (83.9%) of the officials and top officials among the respondents were fully contented with the profession. Among those who were not contended with the police career due to heavy work, a large part (40 out of 46, i.e. 87%) belonged to the group of subordinate officials, and among those who were not contented with the police career due to bad service conditions 91.2 per cent (i.e. 52 out of 57) were also identified as subordinates. Hence it may be understood from this that the subordinate officials were generally not contented with their profession. This may be one of the reasons for the disequilibrium in the police order today. Table 4.23 shows the findings.

Length of service of an officer in the profession as we have seen earlier has a great influence on their satisfaction in the professional career. We examined the data on the contentment in service with respect to the length of service of the respondents and it was revealed that among those who had below ten years of service in the career, a majority (53.4%) were satisfied with the police profession. A still greater majority

Table 4.24

Length of Service of the Police Officials and their Contentment with the Career in the Police Department

Experience	*Length of Service*			*Total*
	Below 10 years	*10-20 years*	*Above 20 years*	
Contented with police career	47 (53.4%)	76 (57.6%)	96 (73.8%)	219 (62.6%)
Discontented due to heavy work	17 (19.3%)	16 (12.1%)	13 (10.0%)	46 (13.1%)
Discontented due to bad service conditions	15 (17.1%)	28 (21.2%)	14 (10.8%)	57 (16.3%)
Discontented due to bad behaviour of superiors and other reasons	9 (10.2%)	12 (9.7%)	7 (5.4%)	28 (8.0%)
Total	88 (100%)	132 (100%)	130 (100%)	350 (100%)

(73.8%) of the respondents among those who had more than

twenty years of service in the department were found to derive satisfaction from police career. In this connection it may be pointed out that service conditions and other facilities which the officers are availing might be far better than what they had at the time of their entry into service at the lower cadres in comparison. On the other hand, the youngsters who are having below ten years of service were not found to be fully satisfied with the present conditions as they are quite new in service. Among those who are not contented with the police career due to bad service conditions, 49.1 per cent (28 out of 57) were having ten to twenty years of service in the department. Here, also it is evident from Table 4.24 that those who are having more service in the department were more satisfied with the existing service benefits in the police department. Hence it is to be inferred from the findings that the length of service and its influence on the maturity of thinking and attitude among officials is very important in deriving satisfaction or contentment in the job situation.

Conclusion

In the foregoing discussion the relationship of the nature of police career and the degree of professional attainment by the police in service both self-assessment of the police and their actual contribution to service have been studied from different angles. We have examined their motivation to join the police service, nature and mode of responding to reported cases, attitude towards investigation, contentment in career and related factors. Major independent variables used in this part of analysis include: (1) official status, (2) level of education, (3) age of respondents and (4) length of service of respondents.

To sum up, it was generally noted that the desire for status was quite common among officers especially among the higher cadres of the police force. The police in Kerala as understood from the present study has been very much alert to its duties towards society. They have responded to offences very quickly. To a large extent the initiative in this regard was taken by higher levels of officialdom, i.e. the police officers. In this regard. age and superior position of police deserves special mention. In general, the police had taken things easy especially in tackling offensive situations and the offenders in general. The special role of the officials and senior officials with respect to the hierarchy of position as well as experience is an important observation of the study. This part of the analysis has thrown light on the fact that the escape of offenders from punishment very commonly occurs due to the change in the attitude of the witnesses. This may be under the influence of bribes or other influences on them. In this aspect the police officers as a whole are united in their opinion. The police respondents, as observed in this study, in recognition of the meritorious service have obtained due credits and rewards. They have been quite successful, according to them, in maintaining law and order within the society. They have contributed much to their professional equipment, ability and satisfaction as evidenced in the present study. Here our hypothesis on the relationship between police career, education, official status on the one hand and the attainment of professional satisfaction and official credits by the police on the other stands verified. The relationship between the above factors and contentment in police career has been well established in the foregoing discussion.

5

THE POLICE AND THE COMMUNITY

The primary duty of the police is to enforce law and order in the society. The measure of success of the police department is presumably some measure of the degree to which it has in fact enforced the law (Bardua, 1967 : 34). Relations between the police and the community are quite unlike other relationships in society. Here, social order, security, confidence and discipline are some of the important aspects of this social interaction. But as everywhere else, in India also police is an object not merely of dislike but hatred (Varma, 1972 : 485). Quite contrary to expectations, distrust of the police is so heavily ingrained in the general public that the first inclination of the average citizen is to keep away from the police as far as possible. To Venugopal Rao, the most important criterion to judge the success or failure of the police in any country is the degree of public understanding of the role of the police and the degree of co-operation, the amount of willing support that the police can obtain from the public in their hazardous and complex duties (Rao, 1962: 190). In short the apparent reaction of the society to police appears to be distorted from the ideal. This kind of condition requires special consideration by the social scientist.

Very often the nature of police functions tend to make police officers feel isolated from the community. The working personality of the police may itself evoke tension in others and result in mutual aloofness. In so far, as the police feel isolated and view that the public is hostile towards them, they are more cohesive and more likely to think in the we-versus-they mentality characteristic of warfare. Only with the support and co-operation of the public can the police function properly in society. In matters of detection of crime, prevention of crime, maintaining law and order under their jurisdiction, etc., police seek the co-operation of the community around them. Hence the real process and the outcome of police-community relations in modern society becomes a matter of great concern for social scientists.

In this context, it would be quite proper to make an enquiry into the actual nature of relationship existing between the public and the police in Kerala, more especially about the feelings of the public about the police. Thus in our sample we examined the police-community relations from the viewpoint of both the police officials and the community members.

The hypothesis to be tested in this context is the following. Effectiveness of police-community relations in society tends to vary with the social equipment and mode of behaviour of the police. The official position of the interacting police and the relationships with the community are mutually dependent. The police attitude to the members and the type of community are related. Self assessment of the police on its approach to the community and the length of service of the officers are related. The educational background of community members and their reactions to police service have a close relationship with each other. We have measured these in terms of education, length of service, and official position of the police. Level of education of community members, type of society, satisfaction of community members with the police approach, etc. were also used for the purpose of the present analysis.

Police and Community

On our enquiry from police officials in the study about their experiences in the matter of police-community relations in their respective localities it was found that a major part (89.1%) of the respondents had the opinion that they could maintain smooth relations with the community around them. It is quite possible that the outcome of interaction between the community and the police may well depend on the level of officialdom of the police and the type of society in question. The type of involvement of the police with the community and the problems faced by the police are not the same always among all the cadres in the police hierarchy. In the same manner, it may also be noted that all sections of the community are not looking upon the police with the same attitude. Under these circumstances it was thought of studying the police-community relations in the initial stages on the basis of the official status of police. Thus, in this study official position of the respondents was found to be an important factor.

Table 5.1

Official Status of Police and Police Community Relations in the Area

Relationship	*Official Status*		*Total*
	Subordinates	*Officials and Top Officials*	
Smooth	215 (90.3%)	97 (86.6%)	312 (89.1%)
Not smooth	23 (9.7%)	15 (13.4%)	38 (10.9%)
Total	238 (100.0%)	112 (100.0%)	350 (100.0%)

Chi-square value=1.06 ; DF=1
Table value at .05 level of significance=3.84

In actual practice, top officials seldom get involved with the general public though they make policy decisions and administer the police force. The officials and subordinates have chances of frequent contact with the public as their nature of work demands the same. Our sample revealed that a good majority (90.3%) of the subordinate officials were able to maintain smooth relations with the community. 86.6 per cent of the officials and top officials also admitted to similar experiences. From the statement of the police it may be understood that there were smooth relations between police and community members.

The educational background of the police officials can influence their attitude towards the public, education being one of the factors in shaping the behaviour of an individual in society. Keeping this in view we examined our data with respect to the educational background of the police. Among the respondents having education up to SSLC level, a good majority (90.5%) were found to be able to enjoy relatively better relations with the community around them. In the case of graduates, 86.7 per cent of them had maintained smooth relations with the community as expressed by the respondents. The analysis showed that there was not much variation in respect of the opinion of police respondents among different

Table 5.2

Educational Level of the Police and Police-Community Relations

Relationship	*Level of Education*			*Total*
	Below SSLC	*College Educated*	*Graduation and Above*	
Smooth	228 (90.5%)	45 (84.9%)	39 (86.7%)	312 (89.1%)
Not smooth	24 (9.5%)	8 (15.1%)	6 (13.3%)	38 (10 9%)
Total	252 (100.0%)	53 (100.0%)	45 (100.0%)	350 (100.0%)

Chi-square value=1.74 ; DF=2

Table value at .05 level of significance=5.99

educational categories in the sample. Details are shown in Table 5.2. The chi-square test showed that the variables did not differ significantly. Here it may be inferred that the achievement of good community relations with the police in society was independent of the educational background of the police as evidenced by the present sample.

One's standing service in the professicn is an important factor in enabling an officer to elicit good results in his career. This is more significant among the police. In close relationship with our earlier finding in the study the views and experiences of the police did not remain steady as one's length of service underwent change. Hence we examined the data on the basis of the length of service of the police. Among those who were having below ten years of service in the department 88.6 per cent of them were of the opinion that they were able to maintain smooth relations with the public, whereas in the case of those who had longest service in the sample, 88.5 per cent were of the opinion that they could maintain smooth relation within the community around them. Only very few (10.9%) of the members expressed that there were no smooth relations with the community. Table 5.3 shows the analysis in detail.

Table 5.3

Length of Service of the Police and Police-Community Relations

Relationship	Length of Service			Total
	Below 10 years	10 to 20 years	Above 20 years	
Smooth	78 (88.6%)	119 (90.2%)	115 (88.5%)	312 (89 1%)
Not smooth	10 (11.4%)	13 (9.8%)	15 (11.5%)	38 (10.9%)
Total	88 (100.0%)	132 (100.0%)	130 (100.0%)	350 (100.0%)

Though the police officials were generally of the opinion that at large there were smooth relations with the community around them, they were of the opinion that the community members were not extending full co-operation. On our enquiry from the officials it was seen that a considerably large part (92.3%) of the respondents were of the opinion that due to one or other reason the community around them was not extending full co-operation to them in carrying out their duties. Only 7.7 per cent of the police respondents answered in the affirmative.

Several views were expressed by the police in this. Few (45.4%) of them were of the opinion that the members in the area were not extending co-operation due to the fact of delay in judicial proceedings and processes. On a detailed enquiry about the reasons for lack of adequate co-operation from the public it was found that 27.2 per cent of the police officials had the feeling that lack of public sense among community members and some sort of reluctance to get involved with the police were the major reasons for not moving fully with the police.

On the other side 19.7 per cent of the police officials felt that the public do not extend full co-operation to the police due mainly to the fear of reprisals from the offenders. An attempt was made in the respondents on eliciting co-operation from the public. As observed from Table 5.4 among those who were having education below SSLC 46.1 per cent were of the opinion

Table 5.4

Educational Level of the Police and their Opinion on Lack of Co-operation of the Community

Opinion	*Level of Education*			*Total*
	Below SSLC	*College Educated*	*Graduation and Above*	
Extend co-operation	23 (9.1%)	2 (3.8%)	2 (4 4%)	27 (7.7%)
Lack of public sense and Reluctance to get involved with the police	64 (25 4%)	16 (30.2%)	15 (33.4%)	95 (27.2%)
Fear of reprisal from the offender	49 (19.4%)	9 (16.9%)	11 (24.4%)	69 (19.7%)
Delay in judicial proceedings	116 (46.1%)	26 (49.1%)	17 (37.8%)	159 (45.4%)
Total	252 (100.0%)	53 (100.0%)	45 (100.0%)	350 (100.0)

that due to the delay in judicial proceedings and delay in other procedures the public were not generally in favour of the police procedures on offences. In the case of those who were educated up to college level, 49.1 per cent of the members were found to have the same opinion. The percentage of respondents decreased to 37.8 when the level of education increased to graduation and above. As a whole it may be pointed out from the analysis that a majority (92.3%, i e. 323 out of 350) of the police were of the opinion that the public around them were not used to extend necessary support and co-operation to the police in their work due to several reasons.

Society always expects smooth police-community relations. Both of them perform their functions in order to have a harmonious set-up in the social system. A slight deviation of one system may well affect the other in its functions. Adverse police-community relations have a lot of influence on the organization and even on the personal conditions of the official. Hence we studied the opinion of the police officials on their personal safety under an adverse situation of police-community relation. A majority (53.7%) of the police officials in the sample were of the opinion that adverse police-community relations will never affect the personal safety of the police personnel. On analysis of our data with respect to the educational background of the officials it was seen that among those who were having lower levels of educational attainments below SSLC, a majority (52.0%) were of the opinion that adverse police-community

Table 5.5

Educational Level of the Police and their Opinion on the Consequence of Adverse Police-Community Relations

Consequence of Adverse Police-Community Relations	*Level of Education*			*Total*
	Below SSLC	*College Educated*	*Graduation and above*	
Affect personal safety adversely	131 (52.0%)	24 (45.3%)	7 (15.6%)	162 (46.3%)
Will not affect personal safety	121 (48.0%)	29 (54.7%)	38 (84 4%)	188 (53.7%)
Total	252 (100.0%)	53 (100.0%)	45 (100.0%)	350 (100.0%)

Chi-square value=20.36 ; DF=2
Table value at .05 level of confidence=5.99

relations will affect the personal career and safety of the police. However, a still larger majority (84.4%) of graduates in the sample felt the opposite. Among those who were having education up to college level also, a majority (54.7%) felt that adverse police-community relations would not affect the personal career and safety of the police. From the foregoing analysis, the emergent finding is that the educational background of the police is an important factor in the issue. Their feelings about the consequence of adevrse police-community relations were found to vary with the level of education. The percentage of response in this context increases with increasing level of education of the officials in the analysis. On applying the chi-square test to the analysis, the value showed that the two variables were significantly related at .05 level of confidence. Details are listed in Table 5.5. Hence it may be concluded that as the educational achievements of the official increase their feeling of confidence in service irrespective of the ulterior factors in rendering service also increases. This may well indicate that the police in the context of increased education derive more confidence to face risk even in adverse situations of police-community relations.

In this connection, it is a pertinent question that in many situations the adverse police-community relations may reflect on the co-operation of the public towards the police. Here it may be noted that the rigidity of conventional procedures, the authority of the police, their behaviour to the public etc., assume more important dimensions in the present problem.

As a measure of the public feelings on the approach of the police towards the public it was found in our enquiry in the present analysis that as many as 90.6 per cent of the respondents were of the opinion that the approach of the police towards the community was far from satisfaction and it should be modified or remedied to the extent possible. When this view was studied on the basis of the official level of respondents it was interestingly noted that irrespective of offical status, the police respondents themselves at large were found to admit that the approach towards the community was far from satisfactory and needed modification. In this attitude the official categories have not shown much difference as indicated by the percentages of responses on the need for modification of police approach towards the community. The details are given in the Table 5.6.

Table 5.6
Official Status of the Police and their Self Assessment on the Approach of the Police Towards Community

Self Assessment of Police	*Official Status of Respondents*		*Total*
	Subordinates	*Officials and Top Officials*	
Far from satisfactory and must be modified	218 (91.6%)	99 (88.4%)	317 (90.6%)
Satisfactory and needs no modification	20 (8.4%)	13 (11.6%)	33 (9.4%)
Total	238 (100.0%)	112 (100.0%)	350 (100.0%)

Police Approach

The self assessment of the police on their approach and the realization of the need for modifying this approach to community may be a function of age and experience also as one's experience in life can very well make him a judge on many practical issues particularly those involving human relations. This is more so in the cases of service machinery like the police. In order to explain the influence of these factors like age on the problem of police-community relations the data were examined on the basis of age and it was found that while 85.1 per cent of the younger age group among police (i.e. 20 to 30 years) felt the necessity for modification of the existing pattern of approach, a still greater percentage (92.4%) of the older age group (40 to 50 years) shared the idea. It can also be noted that there was not much difference in the response among middle-aged people between thirty to forty years in the analysis as indicated in Table 5.7. It was specifically noted that there were only a very few (9.4%) respondents in the sample who had the feeling that the present system of police approach to community was satisfactory.

In close relation to the above analysis the experience acquired by the officials through their service in the profession may be taken to be an important criterion in formulating judgments on professional behaviour. Accordingly the data were analysed on these lines. As shown in Table 5.8 it was observed that 76.1 per cent members from among the beginners in the profession having under ten years of service were found to feel the necessity for modifying the police approach to the community. A subs-

Table 5.7

Age of the Police and their Self Assessment on the Approach of the Police Towards Community

Self Assessment of Police	*Age of Respondents (in years)* 20-30	30 40	40-50	Above 50	*Total*
Not satisfactory and must be modified	40 (85.1%)	132 (92.3%)	97 (92.4%)	48 (87.3%)	317 (90.6%)
Satisfactory and no need of modification	7 (14.9%)	11 (7.7%)	8 (7.6%)	7 (12.7%)	33 (9.4%)
Total	47 (100.0%)	143 (100.0%)	105 (100.0%)	15 (100.0%)	350 (100.0%)

tantial part, i.e. 95.4 per cent of the members having the longest experience (above 20 years) in the sample also maintained the same view. It may be pointed out here that only a very meagre (4.6%) section of senior members of police could feel that there was no need for modification of the police attitude towards the community. Here the significant role of longer service is important. Well-experienced members at large were emphatic on the necessity for modifying the police approach towards society. The chi-square test showed that the relationship between the self-assessment of the police and length of service or experience were significant at .05 level of confidence.

In this connection, it is worth recalling from the foregoing discussion that while official status, educational level and age grades were found to have no influence on the formulation of judgement among the police official in the police-community interaction, the length of service or degree of experience one acquired through the career was found to be a determinant factor in maintaining police-community relations. This constitutes an important part of our study.

Table 5.8

Length of Service of the Police and their Self Assessmment on the Approach of the Police towards the Community

Self Assessment of Police	*Length of Service*			*Total*
	Below 10 years	*10 to 20 years*	*Above 20 years*	
Not satisfactory and must be modified	67 (76.1%)	126 (95.5%)	124 (95.4%)	317 (90.6%)
Satisfactory and needs no modification	21 (23.9%)	6 (4.5%)	6 (4.6%)	33 (9.4%)
Total	88 (100%)	132 (100%)	130 (100%)	350 (100%)

Chi-square value=28.63; DF= 2
Table value at .05 level of significance=5.99

Following from the finding in the foregoing discussion and from the importance of the problem of police-community relations, we thought that it would be quite proper to enquire about the views or suggestions of the police as remedial measures to the earlier findings. Accordingly the data were examined on the basis of the official status of the respondents and it was found that the general demand among the respondents in general was confined to the problem of better service conditions, providing adequate facilities for carrying out the regular work, the provision for adequate strength of staff and avoiding interventions of any kind particularly political from outside. Among the subordinate officials as indicated in Table 5.9, 44.1 per cent (105 out of 238) were of the opinion that only by providing adequate facilities for service could they work efficiently in their field.

By facilities the respondents primarly meant means of adequate conveyance, modern scientific equipment including adequate forensic laboratory facilities required for investigation and confirmation of cases, etc. 39.3 per cent of the officials and top officials also agreed with this view. Among subordinates 33.6 per cent were of the opinion that for the improvement of police service in the state they should be provided with adequate strength of staff. Here 33.9 per cent of the officials and top officials were also of this opinion. It is interesting to note from Table 5.9 that while 40.8 per cent of the subordinates (i.e. 97 out of 238) suggested the improvement of service conditions of the police, only 29.5 (i.e. 33 out of 112) of the superior officials felt so. This finding throws light on the fact that the subordinates were less satisfied than the superiors in matters of service conditions. This may be a reason for the reported unrest among the subordinate police officials. But it may be noted that on enquiry regarding the means for improving the service of the police in the state only 16.4 per cent of the subordinates suggested the selection of efficient, educated persons in the force and providing them with adequate and good training based on modern scientific methods replacing the old fashioned muscle-

Table 5.9

Official Status of the Police and their Suggestions for Improving of Polic Service

Suggestions	*Official Status*		*Total*
	Subordinates	*Officials and Top Officials*	
Sample strength	**238** (100%)	**112** (100%)	**350** (100%)
Provide adequate strength	80 (33.6%)	38 (33.9%)	118 (33.7%)
Improve service conditions	97 (40.8%)	33 (29.5%)	130 (37.1%)
Recruit efficient personnel and adequate training	39 (16.4%)	28 (25.0%)	67 (19.1%)
Provide adequate facilities	105 (44.1%)	44 (39.3%)	149 (42.6%)
Avoid political interference	57 (23.9%)	31 (27.7%)	88 (25.1%)
Total	378	174	552

oriented training. In this matter 25 per cent of the officials and top officials (28 out of 112) had this view.

There is a recent complaint against the police force in the matter of political interference in their work. This may have a lot of influence in the enforcement of law and order in the society. In our sample for the study 23.9 per cent (57 out of 238) subordinate officials and 27.7 per cent (i.e. 31 out of 112) officials and top officials demanded that political interference in police work be stopped for extending their service efficiently to the community around them and to improve the services of the police to the public. From the above analysis it may also be pointed out that only by providing adequate strength of police personnel and improving the facilities and service conditions could the police force enlighten their service in the state. In this aspect of our finding all officials irrespective of their official status agreed with the view.

In formulating suggestions for improving the conditions of

Table 5.10

Educational Level of Police and their Suggestions for the Improving of Police Service

Suggestions	*Educational Level*			*Total*
	Below SSLC	*College Educated*	*Graduation and Above*	
Sample strength	**252 (100%)**	**53 (100%)**	**45 (100%)**	**350 (100%)**
Provide adequate strength	89 (35.3%)	15 (28.3%)	14 (31.1%)	118 (33.7%)
Improve service conditions	97 (38.5%)	20 (37.7%)	13 (28.9%)	130 (37.1%)
Recruit efficient personnel and provide adequate and good training	32 (12.7%)	17 (32.1%)	18 (40.0%)	67 (19.1%)
Provide adequate facilities	112 (44.4%)	21 (39.6%)	16 (35.6%)	149 (42.6%)
Avoid political interference	68 (26.9%)	10 (18.9%)	10 (22.2%)	88 (25.1%)
Total	398	83	71	552

police-community relations, respondents of different educational backgrounds have responded differently. As revealed in Table 5.10, suggestions for enhancing the strength of staff and the provision of improved service conditions were forthcoming from policemen having lower educational attainments. With regard to the suggestions on the precaution against political interference, the higher educated police personnel were found to be more prominent in the sample. Among those who were having education of less than SSLC level, 44.4 per cent (112 out of 252) suggested to provide adequate facilities to improve the service conditions. Whereas 40.0 per cent (i.e. 18 out of 45) of the sample who were graduates maintained the view that recruitment of efficient, educated persons and providing adequate scientific training alone would improve the police system and consequently police-community relations.

When these suggestions were examined under the influence of age of respondents, the analysis revealed that the suggestions of adequate facilities and strength of staff were more from middle-aged (30-50 years) respondents than members of other age grades. With regard to the suggestions on avoiding political interference it was particularly noted that members of higher age group, i.e. those above fifty years of age group were the largest (32.7%) in share. Young officials were generally of the opinion that for improving the service of the police in the state the authorities should recruit efficient and educated personnel in the force and provide them with adequate and qualitative training. Among those who were in the age group of thirty to forty years, a large part, 41.30 per cent (59 out of 143) suggested to provide better service conditions to enable the police force to improve their work and contact towards the community. 44.1 per cent respondents of this study (63 out of 143) had suggested to have adequate facilities. These findings well indicate that the facilities now available to the police in the state are not adequate for their special nature of work in the society. Table 5.11 gives the details of the findings.

While considering the competency of an officer especially in matters relating to the suggestions on one's own profession the extent of service he may have in the profession is an important criterion. Hence these suggestions and the backgrounds of

Table 5.11

Age of the Police and their Suggestions to the Improving of Police Service

Suggestions	*Age of the Respondents* 20-30 years	30-40 years	40-50 years	Above 50 years	*Total*
Sample strength	**47** (100%)	**143** (100%)	**105** (100%)	**55** (100%)	**350** (100%)
Provide adequate strength	14 (29.8%)	49 (34.3%)	36 (34.3%)	19 (34.5%)	118 (33.7%)
Improve service conditions	14 (29.8%)	59 (41.3%)	39 (37.1%)	18 (32.7%)	130 (37.1%)
Recruit efficient personnel and provide adequate and good training	17 (36 2%)	29 (20 3%)	13 (12.4%)	8 (14.5%)	67 (19.1%)
Provide adequate facilities	14 (29.8%)	63 (44.1%)	50 (47.6%)	22 (40.0%)	149 (42.6%)
Avoid political interference	10 (21.3%)	33 (23.1%)	27 (25.7%)	18 (32.7%)	88 (25.1%)
Total	69	233	165	85	552

these suggestions were studied in terms of length of service of the respondents in the study. Analysis from Table 5.12 shows that respondents from the group of relatively shorter service duration (below 10 years) expressed more inclination to have

Table 5.12

Length of Service of the Police and their Suggestions to the Improving of Police Service

Suggestions	*Length of Service*			*Total*
	Below 10 years	*10-20 years*	*Above 20 years*	
Sample strength	**88 (100%)**	**132 (100%)**	**130 (100%)**	**350 (100%)**
Provide adequate strength	25 (28.4%)	51 (38.6%)	42 (32.3%)	118 (33.7%)
Improve service conditions	31 (35.2%)	57 (43.2%)	42 (32.3%)	130 (37.1%)
Recruit efficient personnel and provide adequate and good training	28 (31.8%)	21 (15.9%)	18 (13.8%)	67 (19.1%)
Provide adequate facilities	32 (36.4%)	59 (44.7%)	58 (44.6%)	149 (42.6%)
Avoid political interference	28 (31.8%)	22 (16.7%)	38 (29.2%)	88 (25.1%)
Total	144	210	198	552

added facilities for their work. This special quality of the spirit of service among the beginners or youngsters in service, we have been noticing as a unique phenomenon of the study. This observation on the special quality of the beginners in service is very closely related to our earlier findings. They wish more facilities for work and to create better atmosphere in the system without political interference from outside. Here also those who had service of more than twenty years remain a distinct group in their service. Among those total responses of members against political interferences, respondents with longest service (above 20 years) showed the largest percentage (43.2%, i.e. 38 out of 88).

This is an interesting observation particularly when it was the outcome of experience of more than twenty years in the police force. Hence this may well be taken into account as an important issue quite relevant to the problems of police-community relations. An important aspect of the study at this stage is the quite visible distinction between the attitudes of juniors and seniors in the opinion of recruiting efficient personnel in the system. While 31.8 per cent of the youngsters in the sample favoured this idea only 13.8 per cent of seniors or those with longer (above 20 years) service favoured this. Here it was very clear that youngsters in police service were quite dynamic and professionally more devoted.

Community and the Police Attitude

The relationships between the police and the community around the system are derived and maintained in our society mainly with respect to several internal as well as external factors. This is a two-way process. The contributing role of the police force and that of the societial functionaries are to be specially identified in tracing the mechanism of the above relationship. The traditional concept and attitude of the police towards the community and those of the community towards the police have undergone radical modification in modern times. The police system is an executive and a discipline-oriented wing of the society on the one hand, and on the other it is a service machinery. The very nature of the complex and heterogeneous character and structure of modern society necessitates the police to maintain most appropriate techniques to serve the community in contact.

The real outcome of police-community relations can be achieved only through an ideal pattern of interaction between the two entities. The confidence that the police could build among the society members and the nature and composition of the social organization existing around the police are closely related. Here the degree of complexity of the society and the social equipment of the police unit are also very important.

In order to assess the nature of the approach and distance existing between the community and police, the attitude of the community members towards the police and vice versa were measured in our study. These differences were studied on the basis of the type of the community, i.e. rural or urban from which the members hailed. It was found from Table 5.13 that a good majority (56.3%) of the community members from rural

Table 5.13

Community Type of Respondents and the Police Attitude

Police Attitude	*Community Type*		*Total*
	Rural	*Urban*	
Co-operative and sympathetic	71 (56.3%)	33 (35.1%)	104 (47.3%)
Aggressive	19 (15.1%)	22 (23.4%)	41 (18.6%)
Indifferent and hostile	16 (12.7%)	12 (12.8%)	28 (12.7%)
Others	20 (15.9%)	27 (28.7%)	47 (21.4%)
Total	126 (100%)	94 (100%)	220 (100%)

Chi-square value=11.27; DF=3
Table value at .05 level of significance=7.82

areas found that the police officials were relatively more co-operative and sympathetic towards them in their interactions. The same phenomenon showed serious differences among the respondents from urban areas. Here only 35.1 per cent of the community members agreed with the above opinion. Hence it may be found that the dealings of the police in rural areas may be more co-operative and sympathetic than in urban localities. It was also quite interesting to note that among the community members from rural areas, only 15.1 per cent respondents felt that the police was aggressive towards them. On the other hand, in urban areas the corresponding percentage came to 23.4. Here also it was quite clear that the reaction of the police officials may vary with respect to the type and nature of the community. It was also evident from Table 5.13 that among those who experienced aggressive behaviour from the police, a majority (53.7% i.e. 22 out of 41) were from the urban background. Hence it is beyond doubt that the attitude of the police and the experience of the community members from the police may vary significantly with respect to the rural or urban locality in which they reside. The chi-square test showed that the two variables are significantly related with each other at 5 per cent level of confidence.

In the present study when the influence of the foregoing factors was examined on the variables it was found that these relationships were quite unsteady under different social conditions. As for instance, in the context of our enquiry to explain the nature of the prima-facie attitude shown by the police on the event of individuals approaching the police station with one or other issue relating to basic problems of the community and requiring solutions, it was found that the officials at large (47.3%) were co-operative and sympathetic towards the needy as admitted by the respondents from the community.

However, as shown in Table 5.14 there was a section (18.6%) of the community who strongly felt that the police had an aggressive attitude towards the members who approached the police station with problems of the community. When these conditions were analysed with respect to the educational background of the respondents from the community, it was interesting to note that the more educated people could admit to a benevolent approach of the police. It may be noted here that while only 39.6 per cent of the respondents who had an educational level of SSLC and below had the feeling that the police was co-operative and helpful, as many as 66.7 per cent of the highly educated (i.e., graduation and above members of the community supported this. It may also be observed from Table 5.14 that while 27.5 per cent of the community members who were educated below SSLC had alleged aggressive behaviour of the police, only 8.3 per cent of the highly educated members had this kind of feeling. Here the role of education in enabling an individual to take the judgement in the police attitude may be taken into consideration as a distinguishable factor as evident from the findings on police attitude. Thus as seen from this sample, majority of the educated class approve of the special

Table 5.14

Educational Level of the Community Members and the Police Attitude towards them

Police Attitude	*Educational Level of the Community Members*			*Total*
	Below SSLC	*College Educated*	*Graduation and Above*	
Co-operative/ sympathetic	36 (39.6%)	28 (40.6%)	40 (66 7%)	104 (47.3%)
Aggressive	25 (27.5%)	11 (15.9%)	5 (8.3%)	41 (18.6%)
Indifferent and hostile	11 (12.1%)	10 (14.5%)	7 (11.7%)	28 (12.7%)
Others	19 (20.8%)	20 (17.0%)	8 (13.3%)	47 (21.4%)
Total	91 (100%)	69 (100%)	60 (100%)	220 (100%)

Chi-square value=18.11; DF=4
Table value at .05 level of significance=12.59

merit of Kerala police in this aspect of their attitude towards community members. The chi-square test showed that the relationship between education of community members and the experience of police attitude are significant at 5% level of confidence.

As an indicator of police-community relations we thought of enquiring into the quickness of action initiated by the police on reported cases of offences in the community. Thus we found from Table 5.15 that only a minor part (31.8%) of the community members were of the opinion that police had taken immediate steps on reported incidence of offences. A few (38.6%) of the community members had expressed that on reporting incidences of crimes, some officials used to visit the spot as a preliminary step to starting investigation about the crime. It was also to be added in this connection that 29.6 per cent of the respondents admitted that the police officials used to adopt only routine official procedure on reporting offensive situation.

Table 5.15

Police Action on Reported Cases

Action taken on Reported Cases	*Frequency*	*Percentages*
Preliminary steps taken immediately	70	31.8
Officials visited the spot only	85	38.6
Routine official procedure	65	29.6
Total	220	100.0

There is a general complaint about public that offences or situations of violence are not reported to the police actively and appropriately. This may be true with regard to certain minor offences and offences which will affect the social prestige of victims. It may also be due to the fact that the complainant may not be wanting to spend his time for the hazards of the criminal justice system. The routine official procedures, the mode of behaviour of the executing authority, the judicial processes, lack of confidence on the part of the general public about courts and court procedures, etc. may have influential roles in these matters. Relating to petty offences also the amount of time and money to be spent by the victim may be too much in ordinary circumstances.

Hence normally individuals are not much interested in reporting cases to the police, however, serious and important the problem is. Hence the actual number of crimes committed and those reported to the police are liable to vary considerably. In our study it was found out that among those who had occasions to experience the instance of crime (i.e. 49.5%) concerning them or in their nearby locality 39.1 per cent of the respondents had reported the same to the police immediately. Only a few (10 4%) of the respondents were among those who refrained from reporting the offences to the police. When we analysed this phenomenon with respect to the educational background of the community members it was found that among those who were educated upto SSLC 49.5 per cent had reported cases to the police immediately. Among college-educated respondents, a majority (60.9%) had no such instance during their past life whereas 31.9 per cent of this group of respondents admitted to reporting the offences to the police then and there. Among those who had an educational background of graduation and above, 31.7 per cent had reported the matter to the police immediately. Among them 16.7 per cent of them had not cared to report the same to the police.

Hence it may be noted that in the case of those individuals who had not reported the offences to the police, the educationally more advanced section was more prominent. This difference is almost double between the educationally lowest group and those of the highest. Table 5.16 explains the findings. Here the reasons

Table 5.16
Educational Level of the Community Members and Reporting of Offences to the Police

Reporting of Offences	*Level of Education of Community Members*			*Total*
	Below SSLC	*College Educated*	*Graduation and Above*	
Reported to the police immediately	45 (49.5%)	22 (31.9%)	19 (31.7%)	86 (39.1%)
Not reported to the police	8 (8.8%)	5 (7.2%)	10 (16.7%)	23 (10.4%)
No such instances	38 (41.7%)	42 (60.9%)	31 (51.6%)	111 (50.5%)
Total	91 (100%)	69 (100%)	60 (100%)	220 (100%)

Chi-square value=10.11; DF=4.
Table value at .05 level of significance=9.49.

already mentioned earlier support the finding. The chi-square test showed significant relationship between level of education and the reporting of offences by the community members.

Sometimes the complainant or victim is not satisfied with the action taken by the police in respect of the reported offences. We examined our data with respect to the satisfaction derived by the respondents in the police reaction on the reported offences and it was seen that only 30.9 per cent of them were found to be satisfied with the action taken by the police. 18.6 per cent of the members were not satisfied with the action taken by the police. When this opinion was re-examined with respect to the educational background of the community members it was seen that among those who had the education of SSLC and below, 42.8 per cent of the respondents were satisfied with the action taken by the police authorities on the reported cases. Among members educated up to college level, a majority (69.6%) had no such instances to report. Among graduates in the sample, 13.3 per cent were not satisfied with the police response on issues which needed police service. It may be concluded from the analysis that more educated members in the community were less satisfied than educationally backward members on issues relating to the responses of police on community violence. Details are shown in Table 5.17.

Table 5.17

Educational Level of the Community Members and the Satisfaction Derived from the Action taken by the Police on Reported Cases

Satisfaction of Community Members	*Level of Education of the Community Members*			*Total*
	Below SSLC	*College Educated*	*Graduation and Above*	
Satisfied	39 (42.8%)	13 (18.8%)	16 (26.7%)	68 (30.9%)
Not satisfied	25 (27.5%)	8 (11.6%)	8 (13.3%)	41 (18.6%)
Not applicable	27 (29.7%)	48 (69.6%)	36 (60.0%)	111 (50.5%)
Total	91 (100%)	69 (100%)	60 (100%)	220 (100%)

Community Assessment of Police

In matters concerning police-community relations especially when the police service is looked upon by the community members as a source which will show consideration it is only proper to examine the level of importance and consideration bestowed by the police service on the community. Accordingly the respondents from the community were asked whether they had enjoyed any kind of respect or consideration from police on occasions of their contact with the police. It was particularly noted from the sample that a majority (58.2%) had a negative answer. A detailed analysis of the situation with respect to the educational background of the community members showed that the different educational categories of the respondents among community members did not show much difference in the response as is evident from Table 5.18. This showed that in regard to the issue on modest treatment of the community members by the police, our respondents from the community were quite unanimous irrespective of their educational differences.

Table 5.18

Level of Education of the Community Members and their Assessment of the Consideration shown by the Police towards the Community

Assessment of Consideration shown to the Community Members	*Educational Level*			*Total*
	Below SSLC	*College Educated*	*Graduation and Above*	
Considerate and respectful to the community	35 (38.5%)	31 (44.9%)	26 (43.3%)	92 (41.8%)
No considerate	56 (61.5%)	38 (55.1%)	34 (56.7%)	128 (58.2%)
Total	91 (100%)	69 (100%)	60 (100%)	200 (100%)

It may be noted that while 56.7 per cent of the graduates had the feeling that police were not considerate towards the community members, more or less the same (55.1%) section of college-educated members also expressed the same opinion. It can be seen from the table that 61.5 per cent of the respondents having lower educational attainments also felt that the police was unconsiderate towards the society. This finding illustrates a clear instance where community members derive the desparate feeling that the police was least concerned about the community members in their dealings. This may be an ample chance of strains to develop within police-community relationships.

In the context of polie-community relations it is to be well remembered that mutual confidence between the two units is essential for the normal function of the society. On many occasions the general feeling of the community about police had been one of anxiety than confidence. For instance the people generally had the widespread notion that the police rough up individuals unnecessarily and unevenly in the public service. This is a question involving a kind of threat or insecurity to the life of common man. Viewed from the importance of the situation it was thought of examining the nature of such behaviour of the police in the present study.

Table 5.19

Educational Level of the Respondents and their Opinion about the Behaviour of the Police towards the Community Members

Opinion on the Behaviour of the Police	*Level of Education*			*Total*
	Below SSLC	*College Educated*	*Graduation and Above*	
Police rough up people unnecessarily	41 (45.1%)	45 (65.2%)	38 (63.3%)	124 (56.4%)
No such instances	50 (54.9%)	24 (34.8%)	22 (36.7%)	96 (43.9%)
Total	91 (100%)	69 (100%)	60 (100%)	220 (100%)

As explained in Table 5.19 it can be seen that the respondents at large (56.4%) admitted from their experience that it was very common that the police rough up people unnecessarily on public and private issues. In order to explain the role of education in the formulation of such convictions the data were analysed with respect to the educational background of the community members in the sample and it was found that more educated people were more among those who had the view that the police have an active role in roughing up the people on various issues relating to the community. It may be seen from Table 5.19 that while as large as 68.1 per cent of graduate respondents supported the above view, only less than half (45.1%) of the lower educational category thought that the police used to rough up the people. This finding illustrates well that the more educated people were more able to point out the defects than others.

It was a matter of great concern to explain how the community members have evaluated the services of the overall performance of the police from the viewpoint of societal needs and services. The prima-facie role of the police in society as everyone knows is the maintenance of law and order in society.

Table 5.20

Level of Education of the Community Members and their Opinion on Establishing Law and Order by the Police

Evaluation of Law and Order	*Level of Education*			*Total*
	Below SSLC	*College Educated*	*Graduation and Above*	
Satisfactory	7 (7.7%)	10 (14.5%)	6 (10.0%)	23 (10.5%)
Not satisfactory	73 (80.2%)	50 (72.5%)	49 (81.7%)	172 (78.2%)
Indifferent	11 (12.1%)	9 (13.0%)	5 (8.3%)	25 (11.3%)
Total	91 (100%)	69 (100%)	60 (100%)	220 (100%)

Chi-square value=2.85; DF=4
Table value at .05 level of significance=9.49

Evaluation of the community members as to how far the police had been successful in maintaining the law and order was made and it was found that a majority (78.2%) of the community members in the sample explicitly revealed that they weer not satisfied with the police in establishing law and order in the locality. Only a very few (10.5%) of the respondents felt that the police were successful in maintaining law and order in the respective areas. On analysing the data on the basis of the level of education of respondents, it may be observed from Table 5.20 that 81.7 per cent of graduates and 80.2 per cent respondents educated up to SSLC admitted that the efficiency of police in maintaining law and order in society was far from satisfactory. Here it may specially be noted that irrespective of educational differences the community members had the same reading on the maintaining of law and order by the police in society. The results of the chi-square test showed that the evaluation of the community members in this regard was independent of their educational attainment. Details are shown in Table 5.20.

As there are complaints, appreciations, etc. on the police in the state the actual assessment about the police force may be done only with the amount of co-operation and the mode of service rendered to the general public. Though the police force work on lines given to them by the society around, they may not be fully satisfied with their service if it was not in proper order. Hence on our examination of the functioning of the police service from the angle of the well-being of the society during the past years it was seen that a majority (55.5%) of the community members felt that the police as a whole was not functioning in the way in which it was expected by the society. Only a very limited number of members (i.e. 15.9%) felt that the police function very well in the state. 28.6 per cent of the respondents were of the opinion that the police functioned pretty well in society.

The assessment differed according to the educational background of the community members. Throughout our analysis it was seen that only a few members had the feeling that the police functioned well in society. It may be noted that a majority (55.5%) of the respondents felt that their service was not at all good in society. Only 10.0 per cent of the graduates were of the opinion that the police was functioning very well in the state. A majority (58.3%) of the graduates felt that the police did not function well or rather in a poor manner. Those members having college level of education also agreed with the above opinion in a greater part. The percentage in this regard came to 71.1. Hence it may be concluded that members of the higher-educated group were generally of the opinion that the police was not functioning properly and catering to the needs or satisfaction of the masses in the state. Table 5.21 gives the details.

Table 5.21

Level of Education of the Respondents and their Assessment of the Functioning of Police in Society

Assessment of Police Function in Society	*Level of Education*			*Total*
	Below SSLC	*College Educated*	*Graduation and Above*	
Very well	17 (18.7%)	12 (17.4%)	6 (10.0%)	35 (15.9%)
Pretty well	36 (39.6%)	8 (11.5%)	19 (31.7%)	63 (28.6%)
Not well	38 (41.7%)	49 (71.1%)	35 (58.3%)	122 (55.5%)
Total	91 (100%)	69 (100%)	60 (100%)	220 (100%)

Conclusion

In conclusion it may be stated that the police had a feeling of confidence that there was an effective and harmonious relationship with the community as 89.1 per cent of them have admitted so. In this regard the different official levels of the police did not show much difference in attitude. But in matters of police-community relations the police force especially in the higher echelons maintained the feeling that the approach of the police to the community in dealing with issues are generally not up to the mark and they needed modification. It was interesting to note that they felt this need irrespective of the official status or length of service at credit. In executing the service the police gencrally and especially the subordinates were in urgent need of improving facilities and service conditions than other sections. Here the significant suggestion from the beginners (having less than ten years of service) to incorporate more efficient individuals into the system and to give adequate training is worth mentioning.

In the case of effective police-community relations as expressed by the community members it was specifically seen in the study that it was the ruralities who were more optimistic about the police than the urban community members. It could also be found from the study that in matters of police-community relations it was the highly educated respondents from the society who were more satisfied with the police in regard to their prompt attention to the offences reported and continued action thereon than other members in society. The study indicated that there was corruption among the police. The police had the feeling as found from this study that the escape of offenders from punishment was not due to the police but due to the lack of adequate witnesses and, on certain occasions, bribery to police. As a whole from the study it was specifically observed that the community members at large were not satisfied with the police service system. Only a minor section (15.9%) of the community around the police could find that the police functions very well in society. In this aspect the highly educated members of the society were found to be very critical: only 10.0 per cent of this group could join the above view in the study.

The hypothesis on the relationship between the police service system and the reactions of the community around stands verified in the above analysis. We also tested reasons for failure of the effective functioning of the police as an important aspect of the police-community relations.

6

THE POLICE AND CORRUPTION IN SOCIETY

Society looks upon the police as a source of protection and security for the common man. On occasions when the degree of confidence that police and community build up in their mutual relations, the stresses and strains, if any, that occur within this network reflect on both. However, the results very often reflect more on the society than the police as the society is really in need of police service, especially when the latter is an unorganized body. In this context it is only quite natural that the community, surrounding the police and looking upon the police for service, should be able to imagine the real gravity of the problem of police behaviour. Common instances of problems that emerge from these conditions relate mainly to the allegations of corruption, inefficiency, partiality, favouritism and so on. These are more critical in modern society where the common man is more educated and emancipated.

Police corruption exists when officers accept money, goods or services for actions they are sworn to do any way. It also exists when police officers accept money, goods or services for ignoring actions they are sworn to invoke legal procedures against (Lundman, 1980: 143). According to Barkar and Roebucks most forms of corruption are supported by internal operating norms, socialization, peers and administrative personnel (Barkar and Roebuck, 1973: 26-7).

Under these circumstances it was quite natural to have the doubt about the existence of corruption in one or other manner among the police in the actual implementation of their service to the society. The opportunities for corruption are usually available in jurisdictions characterized by community anomie, segmentation of interest, and culture conflict. Opportunities for corruption are seized by watch-style departments because of the presence of rationalizations supportive of corruption, selection, socialization; evaluation procedures which emphasize involvement in unethical actions; and active and passive support by members of the dominant administrative coalition (Lundman, 1980:157).

The main hypothesis to be tested in the analysis relates to the influences of official background of police and societal role on corruption among the police. The official status in the police cadre and the tendency for corrupt practices of police are related. Officers of lower cadre in police are used to more of bribery and corrupt practices. Employees of shorter duration of service keep away from corrupt practices. Community members and their relationship to the police is very much related to the conditions of police corruption in society. These have been discussed and tested in the following analysis.

Police and Corruption

These may have to be examined for the understanding of the real situation from the viewpoint of both the police and the community. Accordingly when the data on the relationship of police personnel with corruption was studied it could be brought out that corruption among the police in one or other way was quite common from the very beginning of the police system in society. Very often news papers report different conditions of existence of corruption among the police officers. To know more about the extent and nature of corruption among Kerala police we sought the opinion of our police respondents in the matter. First we enquired about the knowledge of prevalence of corruption among the lower levels of the police force.

It was found that largest part (40.8%) of the respondents

were of the opinion that corruption among lower levels was common. Only a minor part (22.9%) of them said that corruption was very rare among lower levels of the police. When we examined this information with respect to the different official positions of our respondents among those who were of the opinion that the prevalence of corruption was very rare in lower cadres of the police service, a majority (80.0 per cent. i.e. 64 out of 80) fell in the category of subordinates. However, a majority (57.1%) of the officials and top officials were of the opinion that corruption was common among members of lower level ranks. Hence it may be inferred that conditions among the officials in this regard vary with respect to the official status of the respondents. The chi-square test shows that the relationship between official status of respondents and opinion on corruption are significant at 5% level of confidence. The details are given in Table 6.1.

Table 6.1

Official Status of the Police and their Opinion on their Prevalence of Corruption at Lower Levels

Prevalence of Corruption	*Official Status of the Police*		
	Subordinates	*Officials and Top Officials*	*Total*
Very rare	64 (26.9%)	16 (14.3%)	80 (22.9%)
Rare	95 (39.9%)	32 (28.6%)	127 (36.2%)
Common	79 (33.2%)	64 (57.1%)	143 (40.8%)
Total	238 (100%)	112 (100%)	350 (100%)

Chi-square value=18.63 ; D.F.=2
Table value at .05 level of significance=5.99

One's age also may be a determinant factor in formulating opinions on corruption as aging and knowledge from experience are related especially among the lower levels of social life.

Hence when this was examined in the present study it was observed that from among those who were in the age group of twenty to thirty years, a large part (44.7%) were of the opinion that corruption was common among lower levels. This opinion was also agreed to by the respondents who were aged between thirty and forty years: slightly less than half (44.8%) of this section of respondents were also having the same view. It was interesting to note in this analysis that among the older respondents, i.e. those who were above fifty years of age, a large number (47.3%) was of the opinion that corruption was rare among lower levels (Table 6.2). Thus following from the above

Table 6.2

Age of the Police Officials and their Opinion on the Prevalence of Corruption at the Lower Levels

Prevalence of Corruption	*Age of Respondents*				*Total*
	20-30 years	*30-40 years*	*40-50 years*	*Above 50 years*	
Very rare	16 (34.1%)	20 (13.9%)	33 (31.4%)	11 (20.0%)	80 (22.9%)
Rare	10 (21.2%)	59 (41.3%)	32 (30.5%)	26 (47.3%)	127 (36.3%)
Common	21 (44.7%)	64 (44.8%)	40 (38.1%)	18 (32.7%)	143 (40.8%)
Total	47 (100%)	143 (100%)	105 (100%)	55 (100%)	350 (100%)

analysis the view of the respondents in regard to the prevalence of corruption varied considerably with respect to age. In this observation the judgment of the younger respondents was found to be more in favour of existence of corruption at lower levels of the police force. Only 32.7 per cent of the older people in the sample could find that corruption was common in the police force.

Educational background of the respondents, as we have seen earlier, can very well influence the real assessment of any situation. Hence we examined our sample with respect to the educational background of the respondents. It was observed that a good portion (60.0%) of the more educated respondents (i.e. graduation and above) were of the opinion that corruption was common among the lower levels of the police force whereas among the respondents who were educated upto SSLC, only 38.5 per cent were of the opinion that corruption in the lower levels of the force was common. It may be seen from Table 6.3 that as to the condition of existing corruption at lower levels of police greater number of educated members have supported the issue. This itself may be a reasonable pointer to the existence of corruption. It can also be observed that only very few (17.8%) of the educated respondents in the sample could admit that corruption was very rare among these sections.

Table 6.3

Level of Education of Police Officials and their Opinion of the Prevalence of Corruption at Lower Levels

Prevalence of Corruption	*Education of Respondents*			*Total*
	Below SSLC	*College Educated*	*Graduation and Above*	
Very Rare	57 (22.6%)	15 (28.4%)	8 (17.8%)	80 (22.9%)
Rare	98 (35 9%)	19 (35.8%)	10 (22.2%)	127 (36.3%)
Common	97 (38.5%)	19 (35.8%)	27 (60.0%)	143 (40.8%)
Total	252 (100%)	53 (100%)	45 (100%)	350 (100%)

In this connection it may also be noted that past service and experience in the different cadres will be a good indicator for assessing an official to a great extent in evaluating his nature of service. As we have already seen it is evident from our analysis that the length of service of an individual in the respective positions will enable one to give a correct picture about the working of the department. We examined the opinion of respondents relating to the prevalence of corruption among the lower levels of the police officials on this basis and it was found that among those who were having less than ten years of service in the department, a majority (56.8%) were of the opinion that corruption was common among the lower level officials whereas only 43.2 per cent of respondents with ten to twenty years of service in the sample had similar feelings. Among the more experienced people (with more than twenty years of service) only 27.7 per cent members maintained a similar opinion. Among those who were of the opinion that corruption among lower level of officials was very rare, only 17.1 per cent of the respondents belonging to shorter service (below 10 years) agreed with the view.

An important factor that emerged from the analysis (Table 6.4) was that the beginners in the career or those who had a service of less than ten years in police career were more critical of the performance of others unlike those with longer

Table 6.4

Length of Service of the Police Officials and their Opinion on the Prevalence of Corruption at Lower Levels

	Length of Serviceof Respondents			
Prevalence of Corruption	*Below 10 years*	*10-20 years*	*Above 20 years*	*Total*
Very rare	15 (17.1%)	21 (15.9%)	44 (33.8%)	80 (22.9%)
Rare	23 (26.1%)	54 (40.9%)	50 (38.5%)	127 (36.3%)
Common	50 (56.8%)	57 (43.2%)	36 (27.7%)	143 (40.8%)
Total	88 (100%)	132 (100%)	130 (100%)	350 (100%)

Chi-square value=26.4; DF=4
Table value at .05 level of significance=9.49

service who might be quite disinterested or disgusted with the problems in service. This should be viewed in the light of our previous finding in this chapter on the critical assessment of the more educated respondents on corruption among police. This observation is quite meaningful in the present set-up where more young, educated and skillful recruits coming to the police system through IPS and other cadres. The result of the chi-square test also supported this view as the variables were found to be significantly related in the analysis.

In the context of our assessment about corruption among subordinate officials in the sample, it was thought that it would be proper to enquire about the corruption prevalent at the higher levels of officialdom of the police hierarchy. Accordingly on analysis it was found that 46.0 per cent of the respondents were of the opinion that corruption among officials was rare whereas 37.2 per cent of the respondents firmly maintained the view that there was corruption in the police at the official level. In this category, i.e. those who were having the view that corruption was common among officials, a majority (80.0%, i.e. 104 out of 130) fell in the group of subordinate officials. As we have seen earlier the assessment of the officials varies with respect to their official position. We have examined the data with respect to the official status of our respondents and found that among subordinate officials 43.7 per cent were of the opinion that corruption was common among respondents at official levels of police. Among the officials and top officials in the

Table 6.5

Official Status of the Police and their Opinion on the Prevalence of Corruption at Official Level

Prevalence or Corruption	*Official Status of the Police*		*Total*
	Subordinates	*Officials and Top Officials*	
Very rare	33 (13.9%)	26 (23.2%)	59 (16.9%)
Rare	101 (42.4%)	60 (53.6%)	161 (46.0%)
Common	104 (43.7%)	26 (23.2%)	130 (37.2%)
Total	238 (100%)	112 (100%)	350 (100%)

Chi-square value=14.59; DF=2

Table value at .05 level of significance=5.99

study, a majority (53.6%) stated that corruption was rare among officials in the police department. From Table 6.5 it is evident that subordinate officials were of the opinion that corruption was prevalent not only among subordinates but also among officials whereas the officials and top officials were of the opinion that it was rarer among official level of the police department than subordinates. The chi-square test also showed that the variables were significantly related to each other.

Table 6.6

Level of Education of Police Officials and their Opinion on the Prevalence of Corruption at Official Level

Prevalence of Corruption	*Education of Respondents* Below SSLC	College Educated	Graduation and Above	*Total*
Very rare	39 (15.5%)	10 (18.9%)	10 (22.2%)	59 (16 9%)
Rare	116 (46.0%)	29 (54.7%)	16 (35.6%)	161 (46.0%)
Common	97 (38.5%)	14 (26.4%)	19 (42.2%)	130 (37.1%)
Total	252 (100.0%)	53 (100 0%)	45 (100.0%)	350 (100.0%)

Then we analysed the same phenomenon with respect to the educational background of the respondents which can influence the formulation of opinions as we have seen in our preceding analyses. Among those who were having an educational level of below SSLC only 46.0 per cent were of the opinion that corruption was rare among members at official levels whereas a majority (54.7%) of the college-educated respondents agreed with the existence of corruption. But among the still higher educated group (i.e. graduation and above) many (42.2%) were of the opinion that corruption was common among officials also. Hence it was concluded from Table 6.6 that more educated respondents retained the view that corruption was prevalent among officials also more or less similar to that of subordinates whereas members having lesser education did not favour the view.

Then we analysed the same phenomenon with respect to the age of the respondents as age of the individual has a definite role in moulding opinion on issues injurious to the society. Among those who were aged below thirty years, i.e. the youngsters in the sample, (53.1%) were of the opinion that corruption among officials was rare. However, this attitude was found to change as the age went up. Among those who were of forty to fifty years of age, 41.9 per cent respondents had the opinion that corruption was common even among officials. Here the significant position in the opinion of the youngsters may be specially noted. Table 6.7 gives the details of the analysis.

Table 6.7

Age of the Police Officials and their Opinion on the Prevalence of Corruption at Official Level

Prevalence of Corruption	*Age of Respondents*				*Total*
	20-30 years	*30-40 years*	*40-50 years*	*Above 50 years*	
Very Rare	8 (17.1%)	12 (8.4%)	29 (27.6%)	10 (18.2%)	59 (16.9%)
Rare	25 (53.1%)	78 (54.5%)	32 (30.5%)	26 (47.3%)	161 (46.0%)
Common	14 (29.8%)	53 (37.1%)	44 (41 9%)	19 (34.5%)	130 (37 1%)
Total	47 (100%)	143 (100%)	105 (100%)	55 (100%)	350 (100%)

Chi-square value=23.10 ; DF=6
Table value at .05 level of significance=12.59

In many situations and more usually in government service one's length of service in the career can also affect the nature of assessment on their service and particularly about the conditions of colleagues in regard to their efficiency and other behaviour. Hence we thought of examining our data with respect to the length of service of the respondents on their opinion relating to the prevalence of corruption among police officials. Among those who had below ten years of service, a majority (54.5%) expressed that corruption was common among officials also. Among those who had more than twenty years of service, a good majority (60.0%) were of the view that corruption was rare among officials. It was also to be noted that among those who were of the opinion that corruption as official level was very rare, a good majority (59.3%, i.e. 35 out of 59) were having more than twenty years of service in the department. In this context our earlier results deserve special reference. Hence from Table 6.8, it may be inferred from the analysis that the length of service of the respondents influence to a great extent their opinion about the existence of corruption among police officials. Those who had less than ten years of service were of opinion that the police officials were corrupt, though the others in the sample did not agree with the view.

Table 6.8

Length of Service of the Police Officials and their Opinion on the Prevalence of Corruption at Official Levels

Prevalence of Corruption	*Length of Service of Respondents*			*Total*
	Below 10 years	*10-20 years*	*Above 20 years*	
Very rare	8 (9.1%)	16 (12.1%)	35 (26.9%)	59 (16.9%)
Rare	32 (36.4%)	51 (38.6%)	78 (60.0%)	161 (46.0%)
Common	48 (54.5%)	65 (49.3%)	17 (13.1%)	130 (37.1%)
Total	88 (100%)	132 (100%)	130 (100%)	350 (100%)

Chi-square value=54.15; DF=4
Table value at .05 level of significance=9.49

We have analysed the opinions of our respondents in the matter of prevalence of corruption among subordinate police officials and among officials. Our next attempt was to assess the existence of corruption among top officials who are mainly involved in the administrative and major executive responsibilities of the police service. They are the people who are taking final decisions and are responsible for control and discipline among the subordinate officials. They are also having control over the lower level officials who can influence them in various matters relating to the duties of the subordinate staff.

On our enquiry from the respondents about the existence of corruption among top officials, 36.0 per cent of the respondents in the sample expressed that instances of corruption were found among top officials, whereas a similar section (33.4%) of the respondents were of the opinion that it was common among them. As to the opinion relating to official career, especially those involving policy matters, officials differ considerably. Hence we examined our data in detail and found out that among officials and top officials 45.5 per cent were of the opinion that corruption was very rare among top officials. 41.2 per cent of the subordinate police officials were of the opinion that it was rare among them. 35.3 per cent of the subordinate police staff believed that corruption was common among top officials also. But only 29.5 per cent of the officials and top officials agreed with this view completely as the data suggested. Details are given in Table 6.9.

Table 6.9

Official Status of the Police and their Opinion on the Prevalance of Corruption at Top Official Level

Prevalence of Corruption	*Official Status of Respondents*		*Total*
	Subordinates	*Officials and Top Officials*	
Very rare	56 (23.5%)	51 (45.5%)	107 (30.6%)
Rare	98 (41.2%)	28 (25.0%)	126 (36.0%)
Common	84 (35.3%)	33 (29.5%)	117 (33.4%)
Total	238 (100%)	112 (100%)	350 (100%)

Chi-spuare value=18.41; DF=2

Table value at .05 level of significance=5.99

Education has a definite role in formulating opinions on matters relating the behavioural positions on any matter. In our earlier analysis also we have seen that educational qualification influences the opinions of the respondents to a great extent. Here we analysed our present data on the opinion of existence of corruption among top officials, with respect to the educational background of the respondents. It was found that among those respondents who were more educated (i.e. graduation and above), a large part (42.2%) were of the opinion that corruption was common even among top officials. Among college educated group only 22.7 per cent agreed with the above viewpoint. Among those who were of the opinion that corruption was common among top officials, a good majority (73.5%, i.e. 86 out of 117) were from educationally lower strata (SSLC and below). Details of an analysis are given in Table 6.10.

Table 6.10

Level of Education of Police Officials and their Opinion on the Prevalence of Corruption at Top Official Level

Prevalence of Corruption	*Education of Respondents*			*Total*
	Below SSLC	*College Educated*	*Graduation and Above*	
Very Rare	71 (28.2%)	21 (39.6%)	15 (33.3%)	107 (30.6%)
Rare	95 (37.7%)	20 (37.7%)	11 (24.5%)	126 (36.0%)
Common	86 (34.1%)	12 (22.7%)	19 (42.2%)	117 (33.4%)
Total	252 (100%)	53 (100%)	45 (100%)	350 (100%)

As the length of service of the respondents increases their attitude towards the profession and judgment about the functioning of the department, etc. will also vary. In our earlier analysis we have seen that the length of service of respondents in the department had a definite role in moulding their opinion.

Hence we examined our present data with respect to the standing service of the respondents in the police force. Here, it was found that the beginners in the department, i.e. those who had below ten years of service, a majority (53.4%) were of the opinion that corruption was common among top officials. But among those who had ten to twenty years of service in the department, only 33.3 per cent agreed with the above view. In this category, 40.2 per cent of them were of the opinion that corruption was very rare among top officials. Among those who had more than twenty years of service in the department, a majority (51.5%) were of the opinion that corruption was rare among top officials. It was also to be noted that among those who were of the opinion that corruption was rare at the stage of top officials, a majority (53.2%, i e. 67 out of 126) belonged to the category of having more than twenty years of service in the profession. Only 20 per cent of those who had above twenty years of service in the department were of the opinion that corruption was common among top officials. Hence it may be inferred from Table 6.11 that the beginners in the department

Table 6.11

Length of Service of the Police Officials and their Opinion on the Prevalence of Corruption at the Top Levels in Police

Prevalence of Corruption at Top Levels	*Length of Service of Respondents*			*Total*
	Below 10 years	*10 to 20 years*	*Above 20 years*	
Very Rare	17 (19.3%)	53 (40.2%)	37 (28.5%)	107 (30.6%)
Rare	24 (27.3%)	35 (26.5%)	67 (51.5%)	126 (36.0%)
Common	47 (53.4%)	44 (33.3%)	26 (20.2%)	117 (33.4%)
Total	88 (100%)	132 (100%)	130 (100%)	350 (100%)

Chi-square value=39.21; DF=4
Table value at .05 level of significant=9.49

(i.e. those with less than 10 years of service) were very critical in their view about the top officials. The general idea was that they were not having good opinion about their superior officials. Whereas the senior people who had more than twenty years of service in the department had a relatively better opinion about their superiors. It may be concluded from the analysis in Table 6.11 that as standing service in the profession increased their attitude about the existence of corruption among police, especially at higher levels varied. The chi-square test showed that there was a significant relation between length of service of respondents and the opinion on existence of corruption in police service.

Police and Community

Among other expectations from the police by the community members the disappointment they face and the frustration particularly manifested through the general complaint about the police by the public was about the chances of corruption among the police. The complainant usually comes into contact with the police, and the role of the police in this situation is highly significant. As such it was very often doubtful that the police took advantage of the situation at times. Thus the public generally were of the opinion that the police personnel were more involved with corrupt practices in services. The direct link of the public with the police and vice versa also affected a lot in the corrupt practices of the police. Hence we examined our data in the line of actual police-community relations.

The feelings of the community members who were considered to be the evaluators and beneficiaries of the police services, were studied. A majority (61.4%) of the respondents were of the opinion that corruption was very common among Kerala police. Only 38.6 per cent of the respondents in this regard disagreed with the above view. As we have seen earlier the educational background of the respondents being very important, we analysed the data on the basis of educational background of the community members. We found that among those who had the education levels below SSLC, 60.4 per cent were of the opinion that corruption was prevalent in the police force. The percentage of respondents increased to 63.8 per cent in the case of college-educated members and the same was found to be 60.0

per cent among graduates and above in the sample of community members. It was thus concluded that a major (61.4%) part of the members in the sample felt that there were instances of corruption in Kerala Police irrespective of their educational backgrounds. Details are given in Table 6.12

Table 6.12

Level of Education of the Community Members and their Feelings about the Prevalence of Corruption among Police

Opinion on Prevalence of Corruption in Police	*Level of Education*			
	Below SSLC	*College Educated*	*Graduation and Above*	*Total*
Corruption prevalent	55 (60.4%)	44 (63.8%)	36 (60.0%)	135 (61.4%)
Corruption not prevalent	36 (39.6%)	25 (36.2%)	24 (40.0%)	85 (38.6%)
Total	91 (100.0%)	69 (100.0%)	60 (100.0%)	220 (100.0%)

There is a popular feeling among members of the society that the actual offender escapes punishment in many instances. This may be under the influence of various factors. We have already seen in the earlier chapter the reactions of the police officials to this phenomenon. As the members of the society are very much concerned with this issue, we thought of enquiring into the feelings of this section of the sample, also. In our preceding analysis we have seen that the lack of proper witnesses, influencing the witnesses, judicial delay and the consequent possibility of manipulations and other processes were the main reasons for the possible chances of the real offender escaping from punishment. But in the present analysis it was found that the community members were not agreeing with all these views. According to them, it was the political influences from outside on the police and other administrative machinery which were the major reasons for the channels of escape of the real offender from police charge. A large part of our sample (44.1%) maintained this view. Only 28.2 per cent of the community members thought that the former causes, namely lack of witnesses, may be a reason for evading punishment. A more or less similar composition (i.e. 27.7%) of community members were also of the opinion that the real offender escapes from police charge and police custody by bribing the police or influencing the police in one or other manner.

As the opinions put forward by the community leaders and the police officials were partly contradicting, we re-examined the data with respect to the educational background of the respondents from the community. The educational background as we have already seen in the preceding pages, has a remarkable part in creating new opinions about the phenomenon. In our analysis among those who had a lower educational background (i.e. below SSLC), 38.5 per cent of them were of the opinion that lack of adequate witnesses may be a reason for the escape of the real offender from punishment. In this group also 32.9 per cent of them believed that political pressures exerted on the police and administrative sources in favour of the offenders were important reasons for such a condition.

Table 6.13

Level of Education of the Community Members and the Reasons for Escaping the Actual Offenders from Punishment

Reasons for Escape	*Level of Education*			*Total*
	Below SSLC	*College Educated*	*Graduation and Above*	
Political Pressure	30 (32.9%)	42 (60.8%)	25 (41.7%)	97 (44 1%)
Lack of adequate witnesses	35 (38.5%)	12 (17.4%)	15 (25.0%)	62 (28.2%)
Bribe to the police and inefficiency of police	26 (28.6%)	15 (21.8%)	20 (33.3%)	61 (27.7%)
Total	91 (100%)	69 (100%)	60 (100%)	220 (100%)

28.6 per cent members thought this factor as influencing the police through one or other means could also be the reason for the above phenomenon. It was to be noted here that among the respondents with college education, a majority (60.8%) were of the opinion that political pressure on the police in favour of the offenders was the main reason for the escape of the real offender from punishment as they themselves admitted to be familiar with several such cases. 41.7 per cent of the highly educated group (i.e. graduation and above) agreed with this view. More significantly it may be added here that one-third of the graduates from the community members believed that influencing the police through bribe, other relations including personal etc. would also pave the way for the escape of the actual offender from punishment. 21.8 per cent of respondents educated up to college also maintained this view. Hence it may be understood from Table 6.13 that members with relatively higher education were generally of the opinion that the escaping of offenders from police charge or even punishment was likely to be due to influences on the police officials and administrative sources by political or other means, bribes, power of personal or familial relations, etc. of the members involved.

We have seen in the preceding analysis that influencing the police through bribes was a reason for the chances of the actual offender escaping from punishment or police charge. There is a general complaint among the public against the police that the police are corrupt in service. Hence this fact was also a point of interest for us in our enquiry.

We thought of examining our data on these lines and especially as to the practice of giving bribe and getting the benefit out of it, etc. It was found that a good majority of our sample (79.5%) had no occasion to give bribe to the police. 9.6 per cent of the respondents admitted that they had to bribe the subordinate officials. 10.9 per cent members admitted to having resorted to such methods with the officials and top officials for getting judgements in their favour.

It is quite interesting to note that among all the educated groups especially among those who were educated (i.e. graduation and above) there were more occasions to give bribe to the police than the lesser educated group as indicated by the percentages. While 9.9 per cent of the lesser educated group had chances for bribing the subordinate police officials, 11·6 per cent of the higher educated members from the society had this kind of experience. While only 8.8 per cent of the members with lower level of education, had given bribes to the officials and top officials, 16.7 per cent of the respondents with graduation and above as their educational background were understood to have bribed the officials and top officials. This observation may mainly be due to the fact that those who are more educated may find social prestige as an important issue and while thinking of evading police charge and punishment they may think of resorting to these methods to escape punishment somehow and may even try to influence the police by bribing in order to escape from the police or in order to favour them in their matters. Detailed data are given in Table 6.14.

Table 6.14

Level of Education of the Community Members and Occasion to give Bribe to the Police

Presence of Bribery	*Level of Education*			*Total*
	Below SSLC	*College Educated*	*Graduation and Above*	
No such occasion	74 (81.3%)	58 (84.1%)	43 (71.7%)	175 (79.5%)
Bribe to subordinate officials	9 (9.9%)	5 (7.3%)	7 (11.6%)	21 (9.6%)
Bribe to officials and top officials	8 (8.8%)	6 (8.7%)	10 (16.7%)	24 (10.9%)
Total	91 (100%)	69 (100%)	60 (100%)	220 (100%)

In the light of the foregoing observations, an important question that emerged in the analysis was : how are the offenders connected to the practice of corruption or bribary among the police ? As they are directly involved in the problem, their opinions and views on corruptional tendencies of the police may throw more light on the study. It was often doubtful whether the real offender escapes from the police charge under cover of any kind of bribery or similar influences on the police for escape from punishment. From the analysis of data with respect to the educational background of the offenders as discussed in Table 6.15, it can well be seen that a majority (52.1%) of the offenders admitted that incidences of escape from police charge under the influence of the above kind were not common. But a section (24.5%) of the offenders did admit that there were instances of escape under the influence of bribery to the police. A minority (9.4%) even admitted that escape from police charge was possible through influences on police officials by way of things in kind.

13.9 per cent of the offenders in the sample could reveal during data collection that political pressures could enable them to escape from police charge. On examining the role of education it may be seen that while 39.6 per cent of the high-school-educated offenders had to use bribe for escape from police charge, only 13.9 per cent of the illiterates could make use of this method in the sample. Thus it may be explained that it was those who had more amount of education thought of

Table 6.15

Educational Level of Offenders and Experience of Escape from Police Charge through Manipulation/Influence

Manipulation Influence Exerted	*Educational Level of Offenders*				*Total*
	Illiterate	*Primary*	*Upper Pιimary*	*High School and Above*	
No instance of escape	48 (66.7%)	78 (53.8%)	26 (40.0%)	20 (41.7%)	172 (52.2%)
Escape under the influence of bribe	10 (13.9%)	35 (24.1%)	17 (26.1%)	19 (39.6%)	81 (24.5%)
Escape through political pressure	8 (11.1%)	18 (12.4%)	15 (23.1%)	5 (10.4%)	46 (13.9%)
Other factors including things in kind	6 (8.3%)	14 (9.7%)	7 (10.8%)	4 (8.3%)	31 (9.4%)
Total	72 (100%)	145 (100%)	65 (100%)	48 (100%)	330 (100%)

Table 6.16

Cases on Corruption among Police Officers in Kerala During 1978-80

Nature of Action	*1978*			*1979*			*1980*		
	*GO**	*NGO***	*Total*	*GO*	*NGO*	*Total*	*GO*	*NGO*	*Total*
Number of police officers actually subjected to investigation and enquiries	31	61	92	18	48	66	19	70	89
Number of police officers prosecuted	—	2	2	4	—	2	2	—	2
Number of cases referred to tribunal for disciplinary action	—	2	2	—	7	7	1	5	6
Number of cases referred to departmental action	10	29	39	8	28	36	12	15	27

*GO—Gazetted Officer

**NGO—Non-Gazetted Officer

Source: Government of Kerala, Administration reports of the Vigilance Department for 1978-9, 1979-80 and 1980-1.

making use of bribery as a method to escape from police charge. Details are given in Table 6.15.

Conclusion

In brief the present analysis revealed that a large (40.8%) section of the sample of police respondents admitted that the prevalence of corruption was more among members of lower hierarchy in police as admitted by a majority (51.1%) of officials and top officials. This was agreed to by a major (60.0%) section of highly educated members in the police cadre in the sample also. It was specifically noted that this observation was supported by a major (56.8%) section of the respondents with relatively shorter service, whereas only a few (27.7%) of the members with longer service had this view.

The general observation was that the condition of corruption at higher levels of officialdom was rare. But in close relation to the previous observation, a majority (54.5%) of the respondents with relatively shorter service expressed the view that it was common among higher circles. In this police respondents who were more educated largely (42.2%) felt that corruption was common in the official level of police. Quite interestingly enough in this study it could be found that as many as 61.4 per cent of the community members maintained the view that the police were corrupt in Kerala. It was even found from the community members in our sample that bribery and political pressure as ulterior factors influencing the police conduct in the direction of corruption in the large part in our society.

Thus the hypothesis on the relationship between the official status of the police and the practice of corruption in police stands verified in the above analysis. The relationship between the community, the police and the causes of corruption in relation to the present problem of the study were also tested.

We have also examined and found out the nature and extent of corruption prevailed in the State Police Service. A understood from the records of the Vigilance Department for the period from 1978 to 1980 the trend of corruption charges was observed to be a declining one over these years. While ninety-two police officers were subjected to vigilance investigation in 1978, the corresponding number was only 89 in 1980. Among those individual cases referred to departmental disciplinary action for corruption there was a variation from 39 cases in 1978 to 27 such cases in 1980. These findings supported our observations in the foregoing discussions on corruption among police. Details are given in Table 6.16 and 6.17.

Table 6.17

Cases Registered and Petitions taken up for Enquiry on Corruption Charges on Police Officers during 1978-80

Cases	*Year*		
	1978	*1979*	*1980*
Crimes charged on police officers	16	7	6
Enquiries conducted on police officers	46	43	49

Source: Government of Kerala, Administration reports of the Vigilance Department for 1978-9, 1979-80 and 1980-1.

7

THE TRIAD

Three major elements dealt with in the work are the police, criminals and the community. Police behaviour towards offenders as well as community members differ to a large extent with regard to various factors like education, family background, economic status, and age of the members involved. Generally it has been felt that, it is the lower income group of the community members and offenders are the major victims of police brutality. In other words the police are generally more cruel and indecent in their behaviour towards these sections of the society. However senior officials in the police department retains a critical approach towards the offenders. They are more objective in their dealings with investigations and the victims, as a policy. In actual experience the youth section of the criminals and the community members are generally the frustrated sections in the matter of their interaction with the police, on the event of offences. There is a notional attitude about the police that they are always based towards whom so ever they interect with. However there is an exceptional phenomenon that the police are reported to be more magnanimous in their dealings with young offenders particularly those under 20 years of age. This may possibility be due to the impact of recent reformative policy of the government towards offenders. In this connection it has been very often felt that the police has been highly prejudicial towards some criminals particularly those who had a history of repeated offensive career and punishments. It is only quite natural that the police can certainly retain an attitude of illwill towards such individuals who were continuously associated with grave offences and punishments.

As an aspect of police community relations the general public are not at all satisfied with the approach of the police towards them. Even the officials in police service are not having a smell of contentment on the attitude and behaviour of the police towards the community at large. This can be rectified to a great extent by providing adequate facilities, better service conditions, qualitative training and recruiting well equipped educated candidates, to the police cadre. Above all the power of red tapism and corruption at various levels of the force are also to be looked into.

An important issue which very often affect the community and justice to the society is the delay that usually occur in tackling with the problems of offences. This can take place through several channels. For instance delay in reporting the offences, investigating the offences, presenting them to the court etc., are all relevant to the situation. On any situation, immediate intervention of the police towards reported offences will invariably keep up the standard of the police among the public. Instances of non-reporting of offences to the police by the community members are usually found more among the educated or individuals who are placed relatively at a higher level of social status. This may perhaps be mainly due to the stigma attached to the police stations or the formalities associated to the Judicial Courts and sometimes to the very judicial procedure itself. Here the main source of such feelings of the masses develop from the sub-standard nature of verbal or real behaviour of the police towards others, as understood from several instances. It is in these relative terms that the efficiency of the police and the image of the police are judged or interpreted by the masses. The satisfaction that the community derives from the police service certainly depends on the positive contribution of the efficiency of the police. In Kerala this situation is rather a disappointing one from several angles of the problem. Even among the intellectuals and educated people the police services are generally not in the good books. This hard core of the situation is mainly due to the traditional pattern of police approach to the society. It is high time that in the context of modernisation and rapid social change everywhere in all the domains of life an important service machinery like police to develop in tune with other progressive developments. It appears that the police in Kerala especially at the lower hierarchy is still in the pigeon-holes of tradition and precedence in their outlook and outward behaviour. The community members at large do not have an optimism in the achievement of effective law and order in society. Even the educated people who are capable of pursuing the situation objectively do not differ from this view. But on the other hand, from the side of the police the major complaint is that the police doesn't get adequate cooperation and full support from the part of the community in executing these functions, more especially with regard to the problems associated to the investigation of crimes. Here an important issue precipitated from the situation is that the community doesn't retain confidence in the police. It is a reality that neither the community or is members strive to attain the confidence nor the police work for gaining the support of the former. Though other external issues like administrative policy concerned or even political influences may be very well operating on these circumstances, it is very clear that the more the system is capable of overcoming the intricacies for ideal service for which it is expected, the more will be the positive result the police can attain.

In this context an important correlate to the situation to be specially pointed out here is the direction of attainment of professionalism among the police as an adjunct to the condition of police efficiency. Every where attainment of adequate professional skill by the personnel is certainly an indicator of the achievements of the system. As a matter of fact the trend noticed in the development of professionalism among members of the police force in Kerala is not an admirable one. Among the several antecedents to the situation a quite prominent phenomena that come out among police personnel in Kerala is that a good number of them have come to the profession merely for satisfying the needs of an ordinary employment or as a wage earning source. Whereas in an ideal situation of a disciplined executive force like police, the society expects honest, valuable, cordial, efficient, adequately skilled and motivated sincere personalities on the service roll to serve them. Unfortunately this is not the situation experienced in our society. However it cannot but to be added that the new direct recruits to the responsible and relatively higher caders who are usually better equipped and educated to the service are comparatively more sincere and honest to the profession. But in regard to the real motivation to the carrer even these sections have to tread a long path to attain perfection. Whatever be the effect of the net contribution of the police to the society as experienced by the beneficiaries, the police in Kerala have been found to be generally contented with the profession. Here the cleavage is between the degree of the basic satisfaction of the masses and the expected real contribution by the police to the community. This gap still remains to be bridged. Solution to such a situation points out to the necessity of improving the police equipment and factors on the lines, indicated earlier. Of course, popularising programmes of more awards, rewards and other distinctions in recognition of the outstanding performances and skills manifested by the police will be strong incentives for them to develop sincere and honest service.

Now-a-days tendencies of malpractices and corruption are found to be common everywhere. The executive is no exception to this. Though from the principle of its very constitution, the police is excepted to be free from corruption, but the real situation is different. Instances of corruption have been reported from various levels of police force. Of course this varies in the nature and degree of its actual dealings. Mainly police corruption are prevalent at the lower levels of the hierarchy in the cadre. Instances of malpractices and political corruptions where, the involvement of the police recorded, are not rare in Kerala. The Vigilence Department of the Govt. of Kerala has dealt with several cases of police corruption. Many a time the police have fallen victims to the conditions of petty bribes or even other forms of serious bribery. This nature of bribery varies with respect to the nature of offence and the status of the official involved. On the other hand, the police generally are not hesitant to grumble that interference from top levels of the system and other sources of the administrative machinery are serious obstacles to their sincere execution of functions. To some extent this has to be admitted to be true. The police generally complained that political interference either from the ruling party or of the opposition are serious headaches to them. In the view point of the police, such involvement of the politicians on police-cases invite far reaching consequences. Very often the police allege that political parties and even the political leaders attempt to utilise the police to achieve their ends by taking advantage out of the administrative influence, the party weilds. This is rather a pitiable condition which is to be remedied, soon or later for the internal well being of the system.

REFERENCES

Abrahansen, David, *The Psychology of Crime*, John Wiley and Sons, New York, 1960.

Adem Thomas, F., *Law Enforcement—An Introduction to the Police Role in the Criminal Justice System*, second edition, Englewood Cliffs, N.J., Prentice Hall, 1973.

Adwani, Nirmala H. *Perspectives on Adult Crime and Corruption*, Abhinav Publications, New Delhi, 1978.

Agarwal, R.S., *Prevention of Crime*, Badient Publishers, New Delhi, 1977.

Ahmad. S.U., 'Police in a Welfare State', Probation India: *Journal of Social Science and Reconstruction*, no.3, July 1957.

Allman, James J., 'The Public Attitude toward Police', *The Police Chief*, January 1963.

Arthur, T.C., *Reminiscences of an Indian Police Official*, Sampson Law Marston and Co., London, 1894.

Arul, F.V., 'Police Training', *CBI Bulletin*, January 1971.

Banfield, E.C., *The Unhealthy City*, Little Brown and Company, Borston, 1968.

Barker, Thomas and Julian B. Moebuck *An Empirical Typology of Police Corruption. A Study in Organizational Deviance*, Charles C. Thomas (Pub), Springfield, Illinois, 1974.

Barton, Michael, *Social Integration and Police*, International Association of Chiefs of Police, Gaithessbury, Maryland, 1963.

Barton, Michael *The Policeman in the Community*, Basic Books, New York, 1964.

Barton, Michael, *The Policemen in the Community*, Basic Book, New York, 1965.

Barnes, Harry Elmer and Teeters K. Negley, *New Horizons in Criminology*, third edition, Prentice-Hall of India Private Ltd., New Delhi, 1966.

Basu, P.K., 'Use of Discretion in Police', *Police at the Cross Roads*, Seminar Papers, S.V.P. Police Academy, Hyderabad, 1978.

Bayley, David H., *The Police and Political Development in India*, Princeton University Press, New Jersey, 1969.

Bayley, D.H. 'The Police in India', *Economic and Political Weekly*, 6 Nov. 1971.

Bayley, David and H. Harold Mendelsohn, *Minorities and the Police-Confrontation in America*, Macmillan Co., New York, 1969.

Becker, S. Howard, ed. *Social Problems: A Modern Approach*, John Wiley and Sons Inc., New York, 1967.

Bent, Alan E. and Rossum, Ralph A. *Police, Criminal Justice and the Community,* Harper and Row Publishers, New York, 1976.

Berkeley, George C. *The Democratic Policeman*, Beacon Press, Boston, 1969.

Berkeley, George, *The Democratic Policeman,* Beacon Press, Boston, 1970.

Bhardwaj, R.J., *Indian Police Administration*, National Publishing House, 23 Darya Ganj, New Delhi, 1978.

Bittaer, Egon, *The Functions of the Police in Modern Society*, National Institute of Mental Health (Pub.), Washington D.C. 1970.

Bogge, S.L., 'Urban Crime Patterns', *American Sociological Review*, 30 December 1965.

Bonger, William A., *Criminality and Economic Conditions*, Little Brown and Company, Boston, 1916.

Bopp, William J., *Police Administration*, Selected Readings, Holbrook Press, Boston, 1975.

Bopp, William J., *Police Personnel Administration*, Allyn and Bacon Inc., London, 1978.

Bordua, David J., ed. *The Police: Six Sociological Essays*, John Wiley and Sons Inc., New York, 1967.

Bracoy, Dorothy H., *A Functional Approach to Police Corruption*, The John Jay Press, New York, 1976.

Bristow, A.P., *Police Supervision*, Charles C. Thomas (Pub.), Illinois, USA, 1971.

Cain, Maureen, E., *Society and the Policeman's Role*, Routledge and Kegan Paul, London, 1973.

Carstairs, R. *The Little World of an Indian District Officer*, Macmillan, London, 1912.

Cavan, Ruth, *Criminology*, second edition, Macmillan, New York, 1956.

Chaturvedi, B.L., *Face to Face with Criminals*, Rocket Books, Delhi, 1970.

Chaturvedi, T.N. 'Police Administration', *Indian Journal of Public Administration*, January-March 1980.

Chester, Pierce M., 'Psychiatric Aspects of Police Community Relations', *Mental Hygiene*, 46, no. 1, January 1962.

Chon, Alvin W., *Crime and Justice Administration*, J.B. Lippincott Company, Philadelphia, New York, 1976.

Clark, John P., 'Isolation of the Police: A Comparison of the British and American Situations', *Journal of Criminal Law, Criminology and Police Science*, vol.56, 1965.

Clark, R., *Crime in America*, Simon S. Schuster (Pub.), New York, 1970.

Coatman, J., *Police*, Oxford University Press, London, 1959.

Coffey, Alan R., *The Prevention of Crime and Delinquency*, Prentice Hall Inc. Englewood, New Jersey, 1975.

Cohen, Albert, K., *Deviance and Control*, Prentice Hall Inc. Englewood, New Jersey, 1966.

Cohen, Bernard and Jan N. Chaiken *Police Background Characteristics ana Performance*, Rand Institute New York, 1972.

Cox, Rimund C., *Police and Crime in India*, Manu Publications, New Delhi, 1976.

Cramer, James *The World's Police*, Cassel Pub., London, 1964.

Cressey, Donald R., *Criminal Organization*, Heinemann Educational Books, London, 1972.

Critchley, T.A., *The Conquest of Violence order and Liberty in Britain*, Constable and Co., London, 1970.

Das, Sukla, *Crime and Punishment in Ancient India*, Abhinav Publications, New Delhi, 1977.

Davis, Kenneth C., *Police Discretion*, West Publishing Co. St. Paul Minn., 1975.

Douglas, Jack D., *Research on Deviance*, Random House, Inc. New York, 1972.

Dubhashi, P.R., 'The Police in Independent India', *Indian Journal of Public Administration*, January-March 1978.

Dutt, G.C., 'Reflections on Crowd Control', *Indian Police Journal*, April 1960.

Dwivedi, J.N., *Police, Power and Duties*, Allahabad Law Agencies, Allahabad, 1950.

Edwards, George, *The Police on the Urban Frontier*, Institute of Human Relations Press, New York, 1968.

Edwards, S.M., *Crime in India*, Humphrey Milford, Oxford University Press, London, 1924.

Elliott, James F. *The New Police*, (Pub). Charles C. Thomas, Springfield, 1973.

Elmer, Johnson Huber *Crime, Corruption and Society*, The Dorsey Press Home Wood, Illinois, 1968.

Enrico, Ferri, *Criminal Sociology*, Little Brown and Company, Boston, 1917.

Eysenck, H.J., *Crime and Personality*, Honghton Mifflin Company, Boston, 1964.

Gardiner, John A. *The Politics oȷ Corruption: Original*, Russel Sage Foundation, New York, 1970.

Gardiner, John A. 'Law Enforcements Corruption Explanations and Recommendations' in Lawrence Sherman, ed., *Police Corruption: A Sociological Perspective*, Garden City, Anchoe Books, 1974.

Germaen, A.C., *Police Personnel Management*, (Pub.) Charles C. Thomas, Illinois, USA 1958.

Ghosh, S.K., *Police Welfare: Government of Orissa*, Home Department, Bhubaneswar, 1966.

Ghosh, S.K., *Police in Ferment*, Light and Life Publishers, New Delhi, 1981.

Gibbons, D.C., *Society, Crime and Criminal Careers: An Introduction to Criminology*, Prentice-Hall Englewood Cliffs, Inc. 1968.

Glazer Daniel, *Adult Crime and Social Policy*, Prentice Hall Series in Social Policy, Prentice Hall Inc. New Jersey, 1972.

Glazer, and Daniel Kent Rice, 'Crime Age and Employment', *American Sociological Review*, vol. 23, Oct. 1959.

Goldstein, Hermen 'Police Discretion: The Ideal Versus the Real', *Public Administration Review*, vol. 23, September 1963.

Goldstein, Hermen, *Police Corruption: A Perspective on its Nature and Control*, (Pub.) Washington Police Foundation, Washington, 1975.

Goldstein, Hermen, *Policing a Free Society*, Ballinger Publishing Co., Cambridge, 1977.

Gordon, Misuer E., *Enforcement Illusion of Security*, Nation 208, no. 16, April 1969.

Government of Kerala, *Administration Report of the Police Department*, Government of Kerala, Trivandrum, 1975.

———————————————, 1976.

———————————————, 1977.

———————————————, 1978.

———————————————, 1979.

———*A dministration Report of the Vigilence Department*, Government of Kerala, Trivandrum, 1979.

———————————, 1980.

———————————, 1981.

———, *Administration Report of the Prison Department*, Government of Kerala, Trivandrum, 1978.

————————————, 1979.

Gouldsbury, C.E., *Life in the Indian Police*, Manu Publishers, Delhi, 1977.

Gourley, Douglas D., *Public Relations and the Police*, Charles C. Thomas, Illinois, Springfield, 1953.

Gupta, Anandswarup, *Crime and Police in India*, Sahitya Bhavan, Agra, 1974.

Gupta, S.N., 'The Role of Police in a Welfare State', *Probation India: Journal of Social Science and Reconstruction* July, 1957.

Hahn, Haalan, ed., *Police in Urban Society*, Beverly Hills, Clif Sage, 1971.

Hale, Charles D., *Fundamentals of Police Administration*, Halbrook Press, Boston, 1977.

Hanna, D.G. and W.D. Gentel, *Guide to Primary Police Management Concepts*, Charles C. Thomas (Pub.), Springfield, Illinois, 1971.

Hansaen, D.A. and T.R. Culley, *Police Leader*, Charles C. Thomas, (Pub.), Springfield, Illinois, 1971.

Hare, Nathan, 'The Ambivalent Public and Crimes', *Crime and Delinquency*, vol. 9, 1963.

Healy, William & Augusta Bronner F. *New Light on Delinquency and its Treatment*, New Haven, Yale University Press, 1936.

Henting, Hans von, *Crime Causes and Conditions*, Alfred A. Knapf. Inc., New York, 1947.

Hollins, S.T., *No Ten Commandments—Life in the Indian Police*, Hutchinson, London, 1954.

Inciardi James A., *Careers in Crime*, Rand McNally College Publishing Company, Chicago, 1975.

Internation Association of Chiefs of Police, 'Police-Community Relations', *Police and Practices*, A National Survey, Washington, I.A.C.P., 1964.

Juris, Harvey A. & Peter Femille, *Police Unionism*, Mars. P.C. Health and Co., Lexington, 1973.

Karve, D.G., 'Police Administration in India', *Indian Journal of Public Administration*, vol. II, no. 4, Oct.-Dec. 1956.

Kennedy, Daniel B. & Bruce Kennedy, *Applied Sociology for Police*, Charles C. Thomas, Springfield, 1972.

Kennedy, J.P., *Police Administration*, Charles C. Thomas, Springfield, Illinois, 1972.

Kerper, Hazel B., *Introduction to the Criminal Justice*, System. West Publishing Co., St. Paul Minnesota, 1972.

Klare, Hugh J., *Changing Concepts of Crime and its Treatment*, Symposium Publications Division, New York, 1966.

Klare, Hugh J. & David Haxby *Frontiers of Criminology*, Pergamon Press, Oxford, London, 1967. The Knapp Commsision Report on *Police Corruption*, George Braniller, New York, 1972.

Koran, Richard R. & W. McCorkle Lloyd, *Criminology and Penology*, Hoit Rinehart and Winston, New York, 1965.

Krishna Iyer, V.R., *Law and the People*, People's Publishing House, Bombay, 1972.

Krishna Iyer, V.R., *Perspectives in Criminology, Law and Social Change,* People's Publishing House, Bombay, 1980.

Krishnamurthi, N., 'What is a policeman', *Tamilnadu Police Journal*, vol. 22, Jan-March 1972.

Landman, Richard J., *Police and Policing an Introduction*, Holt Minehart and Winston, New York, 1980.

Leeonard, V.A., *Police Organisation and Management*, The Foundation Press, Brooklyn, 1951.

Lemert, E.M., *Social Pathology*, McGraw Hill Book Company, New York, 1951.

Lohman, Joseph, 'New Dimension in Race, Tension and Conflict in *Police and the Changing Community*, Internation Association of Chiefs of Police, Washington D.C., I965.

Lombroso, C.F., *Crime its Causes and Remedies* (Translated by Henry P.Horton), Little Brown and Company, Boston, 1911.

Mabel, Elliot A., *Crime in Modern Society*, Harper Bond Brothers, New York, 1952.

Mabel Elliot A. and Francis E. Merrill, *Social Disorganisation*, Harper & Row Pub., New York, 1961.

Macabe, Sarah & Frank Sutchiffe, *Defining Crime*, Basil Blackwill, Oxford University Press, London.

Malaviya, F.D., *Why do not Police Change Police at the Cross Roads*, Seminar Papers (minneo), S.V.P Police Academy, Hyderabad, 1978a.

Malaviya, P.D., 'What is the Police For' ? *Indian Journal of Public Administration*, Jan.-March 1978b.

Mannheim, H., *Comparative Criminology*, 2 vol., Routledge & Kegan Paul, London, 1965.

Manning Peter K., 'Police Lying', *Urban Life and Culture*, 3, no. 3, Oct. 1974.

Manuel, Lopez Rey, *Crime an Analytical Appraisal*, Routledge and Kegan Paul London, 1970.

Mark, Robert, *Policing a Perplexed Society*, Allen & Unwin (Pub.), London, 1977.

Martin, J.P. & Wilson Gil, *The Police: A Study of Manpower*, Heinemann (Pub.), London, 1968.

Martin, M. John & Fitzpatrick Joseph, P. *Delinquent Behaviour*, Remdom House, New York, 1965.

Mays, John Barron, *Crime and the Social Structure*, Faber and Faber, London, 1963.

McCord, John & William, 'The Effects of Parental Role Model on Criminology', *Journal of Social Issues*, vol. 14 no.3, 1958.

McCord, William & John, *Origins of Crime*, Columbia University Press, New York, 1959.

McLaren, Roy Clinton & O.W. Wilson, *Police Administration*, McGraw Hill Book Co., New York, 1977.

McMullen, M., 'A Theory of Corruption', *Sociological Review*, vol. 9, July 1961.

Melnicoe, W.B. & J. Melnicoe, *Elements of Police Supervision*, Glencoe Press, London, 1969.

Melville, W.L., *A History of Police in England*, Methuen, London, 1901.

Milton. Catherine, *Women in Policing*, DC Police Foundation, Washington, 1972.

Ministry of Home Affairs, *Bureau of Crime in India*, Government of India, 1970.

Mishra, S.C., *Police Administration in India*, National Police Academy, Mt. Abu, 1972.

Mishra, S.C., *State Police Organisation in India* Director General C.R.P.C., Delhi, 1975.

Misner, Gordon E., 'The Organisation and Social Setting of Police Corruption', *Police Journal*, 48, January 1975.

Monteiro, John H., *Corruption: Control of Maladministration*, Manaktalas (Pub.), Bombay, 1966.

Mullik, B.N., 'Moral Training for Policemen', *Indian Police Journal*, April-June 1969a.

Mullik, B.N., *A Philosophy for the Police*, Allied Publishers, Bombay, 1969b.

Nath, Trilok, *The Indian Police, Case for a New Image*, Sterling Publishers, New Delhi, 1978.

National Police Academy, Ed., *The Expending Role of the Police*. Seminar Papers, Mount Abu, 1968.

Nettler, Gwymn, *Explaining Crime*, McGraw Hill Book Company, 1974.

Niederhoffer, Arthur, *Behind the Shield: The Police Role in Urban Society*, Doubleday & Co. Garden City, New York, 1969.

Nigam, S.R., *Scotland Yard and the Indian Police*, Kitab Mahal Pvt. Ltd., Allahabad, 1963.

Pandey, D.C., *Police Coercism in India*, Service Publishing House, New Delhi, 1965.

Parker, W.H., *The Police Role in Community Relations*, National Conference of Christian and Jews (Pub.), Chicago, 1955.

Pfiffnor, John H., *The Foundation of Police in a Democratic Society*, Centre for Training and Career Development, School of Public Administration. University of Southern California, Las Angeles, 1967.

Pollak, Otto, *The Criminality of Women*, Philadelphia University of Pennsylvania Press, 1950.

Radelet, Louis A., *The Police and the Community*, second edition, Glencoe Press, Collier Macmillan Publishers, London, 1977.

Radzinowics, Sirleon & Marvin E. Wolfgang. *Crime and Justice*, Basic Book Inc. Publishers, New York, 1971.

Rammohan, P.S., 'Image of the Police in a Changing Society', *Indian Police Journal*, Delhi, October 1973.

Rao, Venugopal, *Facts of Crime in India*, Allied Publishers Pvt., Ltd., New Delhi, 1962.

Rao, Venugopal, '*Crime Society and the Police*', *Indian Police Journal*, Delhi, April-June 1977.

Rao, Venugopal, 'Police Service: Some Compulsions and Contradictions', *The Indian Journal of Public Administration*, January-March 1980.

Rao, Venugopal, *Dynamics of Crime Spatial and Socio-Economic Aspects of Crime in India*, Indian Institute of Public Administration, New Delhi, 1981.

Reckless, Walter C., The Etiology of Delinquency and Criminal Behaviour', *Social Science Research Bulletin*, no.5, 1943.

Reckless, Walter C., *The Crime Problem*, Vakils Feffer and Simons Pvt. Ltd. Ballard Estate, Bombay, 1971.

Reddy & Sheshadri. *Training Police Officers in Developing Society and Police*, Osmania University, Hyderabad, 1972.

Reddy, Chinnappa O., 'The Police, the Public and the Law' in Reddy & Seshadri, ed., *Developing Society and Police*, Osmania University, Hyderabad, 1972.

Reiss, Albert J., *The Police and the Public*, New Haven Yale University Press, 1971.

Reith, Charles, *A New study of Police History*, Oliver and Boyd, Edinburgh, 1956.

Rolph, C.H., ed., *The Police and the Public*, Heinemann, London, 1962.

Rubinstein, Jonathon, *City Police*, Ballantine (Pub.), New York, 1973.

Santon, Wheeler., *Delinquency aed Crime in Social Problem: A Modern Approach*, ed., Howard S.Beeker, John Wiley & Sons Inc., New York, 1967.

Saran, S., 'The Role of Police in a Welfare State', *Prabation India: Journal of Social Science & Reconstruction*, July 1957.

Savitz, L., *Dilemmas in Criminology*, McGraw Hill Book Co., New York, 1967.

Savitz, Leonard D. & Norman Johnston. *Crime in Society*, John Wiley & Sons, New York, 1978.

Saxena, N.S., 'Police Support in the Investigation of Crime', *Indian Police Journal*, July-September 1975.

Schaffer, Evelyn B., *Community Policing*. Croomhelm (Pub.), London, 1980.

Schaffer, Stephen, 'Anomie Culture Conflict and Crime in Disorganised and over Organised Societies' in *Crime and Culture*, ed., Marvin Wolfgang, John Wiley and Sons Inc., New York, 1968.

Sellin, T., 'Culture Conflict and Crime', *Social Science Research Council Bulletin*, New York, 1938.

Sethna, Jehangir M.J., *Society and the Criminal*, N.M. Tripathi Pvt. Ltd., Bombay, I980.

Sharma, P.D., 'Perspectives of Police', *Indian Journal of Public Administration*, October-December, 1973.

Sharma, P.D., 'Police and Community', *C.S.I. Bulletin*, March 1974.

Sharma, P.D., *Indian Police a Developmental Approach*, Research, Delhi, 1976.

Sharma P.D., *Police Polity and People in India*, Uppal Publishing House, New Delhi, 1981.

Sherman Lawrence W. ed., *Police Corruption: A Sociological Perspective*, Garden City, N.J., Doubledey Anchor Books, 1974.

Shoham, S, *Crime and Social Deviation*, Henry Regnery Company, Chicago, 1966.

Shoham, Shlomo, 'Culture Conflict as a Frame of Reference for Research in Criminology and Social Deviation' in Marvin E. Wolfgeng, ed., *Crime and Culture*, John Wiley and Sons Inc., New York, 1968.

Simpson, Antony E., *The Literature of Police Corruption*, The

John Jay Press, New York and McGraw Hill Book Company Ltd., 1977.

Singh, K.D., *Criminal Justice and Police*, Papers for XIV Police Science Congress 1967.

Singh, M.M., *Minimum Wages for Policemen*, Transactions, N.P.A., Mt. Abu, October 1962.

Singhvi, G.C., 'Police Training Perspectives'. *C.B.I. Bulletin*, vol., 16, Sept. 1972a.

Singhvi, G.C., 'What Ails Police Training', *Indian Journal of Public Administration*, vol. xviii, no. 1. Jan-March 1972b.

Skolnick, Jerome H., *The Police and the Urban Ghetto*, Research, Contributions of the American Bar Foundation, no.3, 1968.

Smith, Bruce., *Police System in the United States*, Harper, New York, 1960.

Srivastava, Saraswati., 'Public Image of the Police'. *Journal for the Society for Study of State Governments in India*, Varanasi, July-December 1972.

Srivastava, S.P., *Public Participation in Social Defence*, B.R. Publishing Corporation, Delhi, 1981.

Schaffer, Stephen, 'Anomic, Culture, Conflict and Crime in Disorganized and over Organized Societies in Marvin Wolfson, ed., *Crime and Culture*, John Wiley & Sons Inc., New York, 1968.

Subramanian, P.S., 'General Elections and the Role of Police', *Indian Police Journal*, January 1964.

Sutherland, Edwin, H. *White Collar Crime*, The Dryden Press, Inc., New York, 1949.

Sutherland, Edwin H. & Donald H., Cressey, *Principles of Criminology*, sixth edition, The Times of India Press, Bombay 1965.

Sutherland, Edwin H. & Donald Cressey, *Criminology*, tenth edition, J.E. Lippincott Company, New York, 1978.

Taft, D.R., 'Testing the Selective Influence of Areas of Delinquency', *American Journal of Sociology*, vol. 38, March 1933.

Taft, Donald, *Criminology*, third edition, Macmillan, New York. 1956.

Tappen, Paul W., *Crime Justice and Correction*, McGraw Hill Co., New York, 1960.

Trojan Wiez, R.C., 'Policeman's Personality', *Journal of Criminal Law, Criminology and Police Science*, vol. 62, December 1971.

Vanaganas, Stanley & Jamee F. Elliot *Administration of Police Organisations*, Allyn and Bacon Inc., London, 1980.

Varma, Upendra, 'S.H.O. and the Indian Police', *Indian Police Journal*, 22(3), January-March 1976.

Vijayan, Unni., *Census of India 1981*, Provisional Population Tables, Director of Census Operations, Kerala, Trivandrum, 1981.

Vold, George B., 'Crime in City and Country Areas', *The Annals*, vol. 217, Sept. 1941.

Vold, George B., *Theoretical Criminology*, Oxford University Press, New York, 1958.

Watson, Nelson A., ed., *Police and the Changing Community*, International Association of Chiefs of Police, Washington, D.C., 1965.

Watson, Nelson A. & James Sterling, *Police and their Opinions*, International Association of Chiefs of Police, Gaithersbury, 1969.

Webster, John A., *The Realities of Police Work*, Dubuque Lowa Kendall-Hunt, 1973.

Westly, William H., *Violence and the Police: A Sociological Study of Law, Custom aud Morality*, MIT Press, Cambridge, 1970.

Weston, Paul B. & Kenneth M. Walls, *Criminal Investigation: Basic Perspectives*, Prentice-Hall Inc., New Jersey, 1974.

Wilson, Jersy, *Police Report: A View of Law Enforcement* Little Brown and Company, Boston: 1975.

Wilson, Orlando W. & Rey C. McLaren *Police Administration*, McGraw Hill, New York, 1972.

Wilson, James Q., *The Police and their Problems*, A Theory Public Policy Year Book of the Harvard University Graduate School of Public Administration, 1963.

Wilson, James Q., *Varieties of Police Behaviour: The Management of Law and Order in Eight Communities*, Harvard University Press, Cambridge, 1968.

Wilson, James Q., 'What makes a better Policeman?' *Atlantic* 223, no.3, Atlantic Monthly Company, March 1969.

Wirths, Claudine Gibson, *The Development af Attitudes towards Law Enforcement,* Police 3, no.2 (Pub.), Charles, C. Thomas, Springfield, 1958.

Wolfgang Marvin E., ed., *Crime and Culture*, John Wiley and Sons Inc., New York, 1968.

Wolfgang, Marvin E., Leonard Savitz & Norman Johnston, *The Sociology of Crime and Delinquency*, John Wiley & Sons Inc., New York, 1970.

INDEX